The

Reference

Shelf

Globalization

Edited by Katrin Sjursen

The Reference Shelf
Volume 72 • Number 5

The H.W. Wilson Company
2000

The Reference Shelf

The books in this series contain reprints of articles, excerpts from books, addresses on current issues, and studies of social trends in the United States and other countries. There are six separately bound numbers in each volume, all of which are usually published in the same calendar year. Numbers one through five are each devoted to a single subject, providing background information and discussion from various points of view and concluding with a subject index and comprehensive bibliography that lists books, pamphlets, and abstracts of additional articles on the subject. The final number of each volume is a collection of recent speeches, and it contains a cumulative speaker index. Books in the series may be purchased individually or on subscription.

Library of Congress has cataloged this serial title as follows:

Globalization / edited by Katrin Sjursen.
     p. cm.— (The reference shelf ; v. 72, no. 5)
   Includes bibliographical references and index.
   ISBN 0-8242-0986-9 (pbk)
    1. Globalization. 2. International relations. I. Sjursen, Katrin. II. Series.

JZ1318.G579 2000
327.1—dc21   00-043887

Visit H.W. Wilson's Web site: www.hwwilson.com

Printed in the United States of America

CONTENTS

Preface

The latter half of the 20th century was dominated by two superpowers: the United States and the Soviet Union. As the countries of the world scrambled to ally themselves with one or the other, global relations divided neatly along two lines. The tensions between the democratic U.S. and the communist Soviet Union defined international relationships for nearly half a century. When the Berlin Wall came down in 1989 and precipitated the dissolution of the Soviet Union in 1991, the power dichotomy fell into disarray. The United States emerged as the sole superpower. Democratic rule and free trade, championed by American politicians, spread to countries around the world. By the mid-1990s people began to talk about an interdependent world connected by globalization.

Although the word has been employed by the media quite a bit recently, *globalization* has no one definition. To economists, it can mean free trade and open markets between countries. Political scientists may see it as a governing force that will eventually impose its regulations on the entire world. Environmental activists often claim that globalization is the cause of the earth's deterioration, the catalyst for global warming, and the reason behind deforestation and the extinction of growing numbers of plant and animal species. Globalization is so large an issue that one cannot hope to demonstrate all its nuances and effects in one slim volume such as this. At most, one can attempt to provide a cursory look at the issues most often in contention when the word *globalization* is brought up in conversation. To this end, this edition of the *Reference Shelf* series is divided into five sections covering the definition of the term *globalization*: the state of business in a global economy; the task of governing a global society; the interchange of culture in an interconnected world; and the effects of globalization on science, including the medical community, the environment, and endangered species.

Defining globalization is often a matter of defining its scope. Does it concern simply economic relations, as many writers would have us believe, or does it also encompass the laws governing interaction between countries? And what of its effects on those interactions? Does the American adoption of Asian ideals constitute globalization? Many writers struggle to pinpoint the essence of globalization. Is it a system, a set of rules by which we live and conduct business, or is it a force, a nebulous power that dictates how we interact? Whatever the precise dimensions of globalization, many writers now agree that it is hardly a new phenomenon. In fact, if we choose to define globalization as economic, we will find that the economic interactivity of the late 19th century often surpasses that of today. International migration of workers existed when indentured servitude was the norm in the 18th and 19th centuries. If nothing else, globalization is not new, but our perception of it is. The articles in this book's first section, called "What Is It? Defining Globalization," examine this topic in detail.

It seems that the majority of authors writing about globalization define it on the basis of economic interactions. Since trade, the actual movement of goods from one country to another, is a highly visible and tangible act, it is no wonder that the subject of trade garners a large share of ink in writings about globalization. Business managers and politicians alike have needed to adjust their practices in order to compete on the global level. In business, taking a company to the global level necessitates marketing at the local level. Politicians, on the other hand, must decide whether all this open trade is good for their countries. Should we continue to break down barriers to free markets, or should we impose protectionist measures? The second section, entitled "Show Me the Money: Business and the Global Economy," presents essays touching upon the issues of labor, new technology, and marketing strategies for the new global market.

Section III, "Who's in Charge? Governing a Global Society," looks at the possibility of a worldwide governing institution. The issue is a thorny one; in order for one organization to institute laws for everyone, individual nation states must cede some of their own sovereignty. A plethora of acronyms—EU, NAFTA, NATO, UN, WTO, IMF, etc.—already hold positions of limited power over coalitions of various governments. Many activists question whether the members of these groups have the right to impose regulations on the citizens of all countries when the citizens never elected those members. The term *governance* also implies a police organization. In a global society, who has the authority to determine what constitutes a crime, to enact a seizure of criminals, or to begin a trial against prisoners? Clearly, determining the right to govern the world's citizens is no easy task.

The details of globalization—what it is and how it works (or should work)—bear on the question of its influence on other aspects of life. Section IV, "Culture Clash: Identical Ideologies or Ideological Identities," looks at this issue. As trade between countries brings about a greater interchange of goods, cultures begin to collide. Style analysts differ on the actual outcome of such interchanges. Some people believe that America and its products (such as fast food, television shows, and Hollywood celebrities) will eventually take over the world until one can no longer discern the difference between a street in New York City and one in Taiwan. Other analysts are less worried, claiming that cultures have always influenced one another (just look at the proliferation of Chinatowns in the major cities of the U.S.) and that globalization has merely served to accelerate the process. Undeniably, some cultures are dying out, particularly those once buried deep in the Amazon forests. Culture inevitably transforms itself, but will it homogenize? Only time will tell.

Just as globalization has left an imprint on culture, science, too, has felt its heavy hand. The last section, "What's Up, Doc? Global Science," provides essays on this topic. Some of the effects of globalization on science are extremely positive. The ease and speed of communication helps doctors and researchers to quickly disseminate and share information, which will, it is hoped, aid in the process of discovering the cures for some of the world's diseases. Unfortunately, globalization also brings with it some negative side affects. Deforestation to provide wood and pulp for manufactured goods not only throws off the balance of the atmosphere's composition, but it also destroys the habitats of many animals. New plant and animal species join the lists of the endangered all the time.

Many people helped to produce this book, and I wish to thank everyone at the H. W. Wilson Company. Special appreciation must go to Sandra Watson, Lynn Messina, Denise Bonilla, Sara Yoo, and Jennie Sjursen for their invaluable assistance.

Katrin E. Sjursen
September 2000

I. What Is It? Defining Globalization

Editor's Introduction

I t is easy enough for economists, political pundits, and sociologists to say that globalization is redefining life. But what exactly does that mean? What is globalization? Is it really occurring right now? How long will it stay (if it lasts), and how does it affect the earth, economy, people, etc.? While few people deny that *something* is happening on a global scale, especially in terms of business and the economy, one would be hard pressed to find two people who agree on what that something is and what it will mean for the world in the long run. Some advocates of globalization speak confidently of an inevitable and irreversible process that leaves in doubt only what role Americans should play. Many others, both detractors and proponents, question the indestructibility of globalization and devote themselves to either halting or, at least, changing the process.

Defining globalization, therefore, is not easy. Thomas L. Friedman refers to it as a "system," an approximate set of rules by which to conduct life. His article, "A Manifesto for the Fast World" (from the *New York Times Magazine* and adapted from his book *The Lexus and the Olive Tree: Understanding Globalization*), presents globalization as a replacement for the system of the Cold War, which lasted from the end of World War II until the dissolution of the Soviet Union in 1991. While Communism was marked by division and treaties, Friedman contends, globalization is characterized by integration and deals. As a system, globalization works; it provides relative peace and prosperity, and it should be defended, in particular, by America, because the United States has adjusted to this new system more quickly and more adeptly than any other country.

Recently, however, the movement toward globalization has been countered by an impulse toward localization—a trend by which a new country is carved out of a niche within an older nation state. Nevertheless, commentators have argued that the increasing instances of localization exist *because* of globalization, rather than in opposition to it. In "Too Many Flags?" (from *Foreign Policy*), Juan Enriquez argues that the global trade market allows a small region to break its dependency on a larger nation state. Protection is no longer necessary, and free trade means that a region can get the same rates from foreign countries as a larger nation state commands. In fact, globalization fosters an environment in which secession is favorable. This article does not help to define globalization so much as it touches on the subject of identity. Attempts to define globalization and its effects often encompass discussions of how nations should identify themselves within the structure of globalization.

The first two writers in this section agree that globalization is here to stay, but neither delves into its antecedents. Like most commentators on globalization, they both view it as somewhat new—a work in progress, so to speak. In his article, "At This Rate, We'll Be Global in Another Hundred Years" (from the *New York Times*), Nicholas D. Kristof compares the state of global relations in the mid-19th century to similar relations today and finds that, although the details of globalization may have changed, the world's societies have some catching up to do if they are to be as globalized as their forebears. Viewed from this historical vantage point, Kristof sees that the future is by no means certain; globalization's momentum has been reversed before, and it can be again.

A Manifesto for the Fast World[1]

By Thomas L. Friedman
New York Times Magazine, March 28, 1999

In the winter of 1996, I accompanied Madeleine K. Albright, then the United States Ambassador to the United Nations, on a trip to the war zones of Africa. During the last stop, in Rwanda, she asked her staff to pose for a picture outside her Air Force 737. The group included a Greek-American, a Czech-American, Jewish Americans, black Americans and white Americans. There were Air Force crewmen from small towns and diplomats from Ivy League colleges, and they were all standing there shoulder to shoulder.

As I watched the Rwandan ground crew curiously watching the picture-taking, I couldn't help wondering what they were making of this scene, which represented America at its best: the spirit of community, the melting pot, the willingness to help faraway strangers in need and, most important, a concept of citizenship based on allegiance to an idea rather than to a tribe. As a picture, it represented everything that Rwanda was not.

And as I stood there, I started to get mad—not just about the tragedy in Africa but also about a budget debate that was then going on in Congress. We have something tremendously special in America, I thought, but if we want to preserve it, we have to pay for it and nurture it. Yet, when I listened to the infamous 1994 class of freshman Republicans—and when I hear echoes today, with the likes of the House majority leader, Dick Armey, boasting that he has traveled abroad only once—I heard mean-spirited voices, voices for whom the American Government was some kind of evil enemy. I heard men and women who insisted that the market alone should rule. And I heard lawmakers who seemed to believe that America had no special responsibility for maintaining global institutions and stabilizing an international system that benefits us more than any other country. And as I thought about all this on the tarmac of Kigali airport, I said to myself: "Well, my freshman Republican friends, come to Africa. It's a freshman Republican's paradise." Yes sir, nobody in Liberia pays taxes. There's no gun control in Angola. There's no welfare as we know it in Burundi and no big government to interfere with the market in Rwanda.

---

1. Article by Thomas L. Friedman from the *New York Times*, March 28, 1999. Copyright ©
New York Times. Reprinted with permission.

But a lot of their people sure wish there were. Like the desk clerk in Luanda, Angola, who looked at me as if I were nuts when I asked her if it was safe to take a walk three blocks from the hotel, down the main street of the capital in the middle of the day. "No, no, no," she shook her head not safe." I'll bet she wouldn't mind paying some taxes for 100,000 more police officers.

And then there was the Liberian radio reporter who demanded to know why the Marines came to Liberia after the civil war broke out in 1989, evacuated only the United States citizens and then left. "We all thought, 'The Marines are coming, we will be saved,' he said. 'How could they leave?'" Poor guy, his country has no marines to rescue him. I'll bet he wouldn't mind paying some taxes for a few good men.

Employers don't have to fret about those pesky worker-safety rules in Angola, let alone services for the handicapped. The 70,000 Angolans who have had limbs blown off by land mines get by just fine on their own. You can see them limping around the streets of Luanda in Fellini-esque contortions, hustling for food and using tree limbs as a substitute for the human variety. And in Rwanda and Burundi, no one is asked to pay for Head Start, Medicaid, national service or student-loan programs. Instead they just have a Darwinian competition for scarce land, energy and water, with Tutsi and Hutu tribesmen taking turns downsizing one another to grab more resources for themselves.

Many in Congress are reluctant to go on trips abroad. They think it looks bad to their constituents.

Many in Congress are reluctant to go on trips abroad. They think it looks bad to their constituents. Too bad. They want all the respect and benefits that come with being an American in today's world, but without any of the sacrifices and obligations that go with it. They should come to war-torn Africa and get a real taste of what happens to countries where there is no sense of community, no sense that people owe their government anything, no sense that anyone is responsible for anyone else, and where the rich have to live behind high walls and tinted windows, while the poor are left to the tender mercies of the marketplace.

I don't want to live in such a country, or such a world. It is not only wrong, it will become increasingly dangerous. Designing ways to avoid that should be at the heart of American domestic and foreign policy. Unfortunately, neither the Democrats nor the Republicans are thinking in those terms. They behave as if the world is now safe for us to be both insular and mindlessly partisan. To the extent that there is serious discussion about a shared national interest, it is about whether we can define a new common threat—Iraq, China,

Russia—and not a new common mission. The "big enemy" is still the organizing principle of American internationalism, not the "big opportunity"—let alone "the big responsibility."

America does have a bipartisan national interest to pursue, and it has an enormous role to play. But we won't begin to fully grasp that until we understand that we are in a new international system. For the last 10 years we've been talking about "the post-cold-war world." We've described the world by what it isn't—it's not the cold war—because we don't know what it is. Well, what it is is a new international system called globalization. Globalization is not just a trend, not just a phenomenon, not just an economic fad. It is the international system that has replaced the cold-war system. And like the cold-war system, globalization has its own rules, logic, structures and characteristics.

Unlike the cold-war system, which was largely static, globalization involves the integration of free markets, nation-states and information technologies to a degree never before witnessed, in a way that is enabling individuals, corporations and countries to

---

If all the threats and opportunities of the cold-war system grew out of "division," all the threats and opportunities of the globalization system grow out of "integration."

---

reach around the world farther, faster, deeper and cheaper than ever. It is also producing a powerful backlash from those brutalized or left behind.

If all the threats and opportunities of the cold-war system grew out of "division," all the threats and opportunities of the globalization system grow out of "integration." The symbol of the cold-war system was a wall, which divided everyone. The symbol of the globalization system is the World Wide Web, which unites everyone. In the cold war we reached for the hot line between the White House and the Kremlin—a symbol that we were all divided but at least someone, the two superpowers, were in charge. In the era of globalization we reach for the Internet—a symbol that we are all connected but nobody is in charge.

If the cold war had been a sport, it would have been sumo wrestling, says Michael Mandelbaum, a foreign affairs expert at Johns Hopkins University. "It would be two big fat guys in a ring, with all sorts of posturing and rituals and stomping of feet, but actually very little contact until the end of the match, when there is a brief moment of shoving and the loser gets pushed out of the ring, but nobody gets killed."

If globalization were a sport, it would be the 100-yard dash, over and over and over. And no matter how many times you win, you have to race again the next day. And if you lose by just a hundredth of a second it can be as if you lost by an hour.

The driving idea behind globalization is free-market capitalism. The more you let market forces rule and the more you open your economy to free trade and competition, the more efficient and flourishing your economy will be. Globalization means the spread of free-market capitalism to virtually every country in the world.

The defining document of the cold-war system was the Treaty. The defining document of the globalization system is the Deal. While the defining measurement of the cold war was weight, the defining mea-

---

As the country that benefits most from global economic integration, we have the responsibility of making sure that this new system is sustainable.

---

surement of the globalization system is speed—in commerce, travel, communication and innovation. The cold war was about Einstein's mass-energy equation, $E=mc^2$. Globalization is about Moore's Law, which states that the computing power of silicon chips will double every 18 months.

The cold-war system was built around nation-states, and it was balanced by two superpowers: the United States and the Soviet Union. The globalization system is built around three balances that overlap and affect one another. One is the traditional balance between states and states. The next is the balance between states and "supermarkets"—the huge global stock and bond markets. (The United States can destroy you by dropping bombs, and the supermarkets can destroy you by downgrading your bonds.)

The last is the balance between states and "super-empowered individuals." Because globalization has brought down the walls that limited the movement and reach of people, and because it has simultaneously wired the world into networks, it gives more power to individuals than ever before to directly influence markets and nation-states. For instance, Osama bin Laden, the Saudi millionaire with his own global network (Jihad Online), declared war on America, and the Air Force had to launch cruise missiles at him. We launched cruise missiles at an individual—as though he were another nation-state.

As the country that benefits most from global economic integration, we have the responsibility of making sure that this new system is sustainable. This is particularly important at a time when the world has been—and will continue to be—rocked by economic crises that can spread rapidly from one continent to another. America has had 200 years to invent, regenerate and calibrate the balances that keep markets free without their becoming monsters. We have the tools to make a difference. We have an interest in making a difference. And we have the responsibility to make a difference.

Sustaining globalization is our overarching national interest. The political party that understands that first, the one that comes up with the most coherent, credible and imaginative platform for pursuing it, is the party that will own the real bridge to the future.

Designing a strategy to promote sustainable globalization at home and abroad is no easy task. And it is made even more complicated by the effects of globalization, which have intensified the world's long-running love-hate relationship with America. For the moment, America has many of the most sought-after goods, services and innovations in the global market. What people thought was American decline in the 1980's was actually America adjusting to the new system before anyone else. We're already around the second turn before some others have laced up their shoes. Globalization-is-U.S.

Because we are the biggest beneficiaries and drivers of globalization, we are unwittingly putting enormous pressure on the rest of the world. Americans may think their self-portrait is Grant Wood's "American Gothic," the strait-laced couple, pitchfork in hand, standing stoically outside the barn. But to the rest of the world, Americans actually look like some wild, multicolored Andy Warhol print.

To the rest of the world, American Gothic is actually two 20-something software engineers who come into your country wearing beads and sandals, with rings in their noses and paint on their toes. They kick down your front door, overturn everything in the house, stick a Big Mac in your mouth, fill your kids with ideas you never had or can't understand, slam a cable box onto your television, lock in the channel to MTV, plug an Internet connection into your computer and tell you, "Download or die."

We Americans are the apostles of the Fast World, the prophets of the free market and the high priests of high tech. We want "enlargement" of both our values and our Pizza Huts. We want the world to follow our lead and become democratic and capitalistic, with a Web site in every pot, a Pepsi on every lip, Microsoft Windows in every computer and with everyone, everywhere, pumping their own gas.

No wonder, therefore, that resentment of America is on the rise globally. In 1996 I visited Teheran and stayed in the Homa Hotel. The first thing I noticed was that above the front door in the lobby were the words "Down With U.S.A." It wasn't a banner. It wasn't graffiti. It was tiled into the wall. A short time later, I noticed that Iran's mullahs had begun calling America something other than the "Great Satan." They had begun calling it "the capital of global arrogance."

The Iranian leadership had grasped the important distinction between "global arrogance" and old-fashioned notions of imperialism, when one country physically occupies another. Global arrogance is when your culture and economic clout are so powerful and widely diffused that you don't need to occupy other people to influence their lives. Well, guess what? The Iranians aren't the only ones talking about America as "the capital of global arrogance." The French, Germans, Japanese, Indonesians, Indians and Russians also call us that now.

In most countries, people can no longer distinguish between American power, American exports, American cultural assaults, American cultural exports and plain old globalization.

The trick for America is to lead without being too overbearing, to be generous without overextending ourselves and to be tough without engendering too much resentment.

Martin Indyk likes to tell the story of when, as Ambassador to Israel, he was called upon to open the first McDonald's in Jerusalem. McDonald's gave him a colorful baseball hat to wear, with the golden arches on it, so he would be properly attired as he ate the ceremonial first Big Mac in Jerusalem—with Israel Television filming every bite for the evening news. At that moment, an Israeli teenager walked up to him, carrying his own McDonald's hat, which he handed to Ambassador Indyk with a pen and asked: "Are you the Ambassador? Can I have your autograph?" Somewhat sheepishly, Ambassador Indyk replied: "Sure. I've never been asked for my autograph before."

As the Ambassador prepared to sign his name, the Israeli teenager said to him, "Wow, what's it like to be the ambassador from McDonald's, going around the world opening McDonald's restaurants everywhere?"

Ambassador Indyk looked at the Israeli youth and said, "No, no. I'm the American Ambassador—not the ambassador from McDonald's!" Ambassador Indyk described what happened next: "I said to him, 'Does this mean you don't want my autograph?' And the kid said, 'No, I don't want your autograph,' and he took his hat back and walked away."

Oh, well. The trick for America is to lead without being too overbearing, to be generous without overextending ourselves and to be tough without engendering too much resentment. But how?

First, forget about the political labels from the cold-war system. Democrats and Republicans, liberals and conservatives; these terms are meaningless today. Instead, to locate yourself and your opponents in the new era, consider the accompanying chart of globalization identities.

The line across the middle from left to right describes how you feel about globalization. At the far

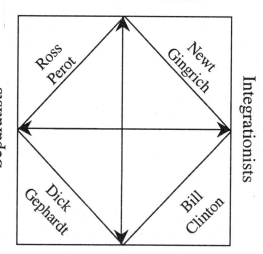

Let-Them-Eat-Cakers

Social-Safety-Netters

right end of this line are the "Integrationists." These are the people who really welcome globalization because they think it is either good or inevitable and want to see it promoted through more free trade, more Internet commerce, more networking of schools, communities and businesses, so that we can have global integration across 24 time zones and into cyberspace.

At the far left end of the globalization line are the "Separatists." These are people who believe that free trade and technological integration are neither good nor inevitable, because they widen income gaps, lead to jobs being sent abroad, homogenize cultures into global mush and lead to life being controlled by distant, faceless market forces. They want to cut off and kill globalization now.

So the first thing you have to do is locate yourself somewhere on this line. Are you a Separatist? An Integrationist? Or something in between?

Now look at the line running from top to bottom of the matrix. This is the distribution axis. It represents what sort of policies you believe governments should adopt to go along with globalization.

At the lower end of this line are the "Social-Safety-Netters." These are people who believe that globalization will be sustainable only if it is democratized, in both the economic and the political sense.

Obviously, not everyone agrees with this approach. That's why at the other extreme from the Social-Safety-Netters are the "Let-Them-Eat-Cakers." These are people who believe that globalization is essentially winner-take-all, loser-take-care-of-yourself. They want to shrink government, taxes and safety nets, and let people reap the fruits of their own labor or pay the price of their own ineptitude.

So next you have to locate yourself on this distribution axis. Are you a Social Safety-Netter? Are you a Let-Them-Eat-Caker? Or something in between?

Bill Clinton is an Integrationist Social-Safety-Netter. Newt Gingrich, the former Speaker of the House, was an Integrationist Let-Them-Eat-Caker. That's why Clinton and Gingrich were always

---

> *The first thing a politics of sustainable globalization must include is a picture of the world, because no policy is sustainable without a public that understands why it's necessary.*

---

allies on free trade but opponents on Social Security-welfare spending. The House minority leader, Dick Gephardt, is a Separatist Social-Safety-Netter, while Ross Perot is a Separatist Let-Them-Eat-Caker. That's why Gephardt and Perot were allies in their opposition to Nafta but enemies on Social Security and welfare.

Al Gore and George W. Bush are interesting hybrids. Gore is an Integrationist Social-Safety-Netter, but not on the extreme end of either. He has certain Gephardtist leanings when it comes to free-trade issues that might alienate his labor-union base. Bush is an Integrationist Let-Them-Eat-Caker, but also not on the extreme end of either. He has certain Clintonite leanings on education, training and social spending that should appeal to centrist voters.

I'm an extreme Integrationist Social-Safety-Netter. I believe you dare not be a globalizer without being a safety-netter and social democrat, because if you don't equip the have-nots, know-nots and turtles to survive in the new system, they will eventually produce a backlash that will choke off your country from the world. And I believe you dare not be a safety-netter or social democrat without being a globalizer, because without ever-increasing integration, you will never generate the incomes and absorb the technologies needed to keep standards of living rising.

But what does it mean to be an Integrationist Social-Safety-Netter? I think it means articulating a politics, geo-economics and geo-politics of sustainable globalization.

Politics

The first thing a politics of sustainable globalization must include is a picture of the world, because no policy is sustainable without a public that understands why it's necessary. This is particularly true with globalization, because the people who are hurt by it know exactly who they are, but the people who benefit from it tend not to understand that at all. After World War II, successive Presidents instructed Americans about the One Big Thing in the world that would be at the center of American politics—containing Communism. Today, globalization and rapid technological change are that Big Thing. And that means virtually every aspect of national policy—health care, welfare, education, job training, the environment, market regulation, Social Security, free-trade expansion and military strategy needs to be adjusted so that we get the most out of the globalization system and cushion its worst aspects.

For instance, a politics of sustainable globalization would have to include a strategy for giving as many people as possible a financial stake in the Fast World. Whenever I think about this, I always recall a story that a Russian journalist, Aleksei Pushkov, told me back in April 1995 about one of his neighbors in Moscow. "He was this poor driver who lived in the apartment off the entryway. Every Friday night he would get drunk and sing along—over and over in a very loud voice—with two English songs: "Happy Nation" and "All She Wants Is Another Baby." He had no idea what the words meant. When he got really drunk, he'd start beating his wife and she would start screaming. He was driving us crazy. I wanted to throw a grenade at him.

"Anyway," Pushkov continued, "about eight months ago, I don't know how, he got a share in a small car-repair shop. Since then, no more "Happy Nation," no more singing all night, no more beating his wife. He leaves every morning at 8:30 for work and he is satisfied. He knows he has some prospects in life now. My wife said to me the other day, "Hey, look at Happy Nation"—that's what we call him—he's an owner now."

Integrationist Social-Safety-Netters feel that there are a lot of things we can do to democratize globalization economically, promote social stability and prevent our own society from drifting even further into high walls and tinted windows. These measures need not be all that expensive, nor do they have to involve radical income redistribution—or lavish welfare programs that violate the basic, neoliberal free-market rules of the system.

To that end, I believe that each Administration should offer an annual piece of legislation that I would call the Rapid Change Opportunity Act. It would accompany whatever integrationist policy the White House is pursuing that year—whether it be NAFTA expansion or most-favored-nation status for China. The act would vary each year, but its goal would be to create both the reality and perception that the Government understands that globalization spreads its blessings unevenly, and therefore the Government is constantly going to be adjusting its safety nets and trampolines to get as many people as possible up to speed for the Fast World.

Last year, my Rapid Change Opportunity Act would have included: pilot projects for public employment of temporarily displaced workers; tax breaks for severance pay for displaced workers; free government-provided resume consultation for anyone who loses a job, a further extension of the Kassebaum-Kennedy act, so that laid-off workers could keep their health insurance polices longer, and a national advertising campaign for one of the best, but most under-reported, bipartisan achievements of the Clinton era: the Workforce Investment Act.

Signed in August 1998, the act brought together and energized all the Government's job-training programs, including individual training accounts that workers can use for any training they believe will most advance their job opportunities, one-stop career centers for every job-training program and an increase in youth training programs by $1.2 billion over five years.

I would also include, in the Rapid Change Opportunity Act, increased lending to Asian, African and Latin American development banks to promote training of women, micro-lending to women and environmental cleanup. I'd also like to see an increase in financing for the International Labor Organization's new initiative for creating alternatives to child labor in countries where children are most abused. It's true: a hand-up really is better than a handout.

Even if we waste some money on these hand-up programs, the Rapid Change Opportunity Act would be a tiny price to pay for maintaining the social cohesion and political consensus for integration and free trade. Our motto should be: "Protection, Not Protectionism. Cushions, Not Walls. Floors, Not Ceilings."

Geo-Economics

I once wrote a fantasy about global investing that went something like this: I brushed up on my German and bought some German corporate bonds. I studied a little Japanese and picked up a few stocks on the Nikkei. I got a tip from a waiter at my local "House of Hunan" and bought a few shares on the Shanghai Stock Exchange. My broker tried to sell me some Lebanese bonds, but I told him that I already had wallpaper. I even did my thing for Russian reform by brushing up on the Cyrillic alphabet and buying a few Russian T-bills.

But after all this, I discovered that I had forgotten two little English words, "Alan Greenspan." Because when the Fed Chairman suddenly raised United States interest rates in the mid-1990s—making the extra interest investors were getting on foreign bonds less attractive—everyone started dumping securities in these foreign markets and bringing their money home. I got creamed. I was a bad lender, chasing higher rates of return without regard to risk.

Over the years I got a little smarter and became a better lender. I started doing my global investing through a mutual fund. A short time after Russia's economy went into a tailspin, in August 1998, I got a letter from that fund—Tweedy, Browne Global Value—reporting that its profits were down a bit because of the turmoil in international markets triggered by Russia's default. However, the fund was not down as much as many others because it had stayed away from Russia. The letter said of Russia that Tweedy "cannot understand investing in countries with little political stability, no laws protecting investors and a currency that may be put to better use as Kleenex." Yes, the Tweedy letter added, in the prior two or three years the Russian market increased fivefold, and then overnight lost 80 percent of its value—a complete round trip." Russia, it turns out, was a bad borrower.

I tell these two stories because they capture in microcosm the two biggest threats to today's global financial system—crises triggered by "bad lenders" and crises triggered by "bad borrowers." Just as there are drug users and drug pushers, in global economics there are bad borrowers, like Russia, and bad lenders, like myself. We need to address both.

Let's start with bad borrowers. I believe globalization did us all a favor by melting down the economies of Thailand, Korea, Malaysia, Indonesia, Mexico, Russia and Brazil in the 1990s, because it laid bare a lot of rotten practices in countries that had prematurely globalized. People keep referring to what happened in countries like Indonesia as an economic "crisis." Well, excuse me, but I don't consider the downfall of the most corrupt, venal, greedy, ruling family in the world—the Suhartos—a crisis. People talk about Indonesia or Russia or Thailand as if they had these charming, efficient and equitable financial systems before big bad globalization came along. Hogwash! Globalization simply exposed a bunch of flimflam regimes and crony-capitalist systems that were not up to the demands of the global system. The real crisis in these countries is not economic, it's political.

The tragedy is that globalization flattened not only the crony capitalists but also a lot of little folks who were just working hard and playing by the local rules (however flawed). In the new geo-economics, we now have an opportunity to assist the innocent victims by helping their countries get up to speed. The only lasting way to do it, though, is to encourage them to become not just emerging markets but also "emerging societies" (like Poland, Hungary and Taiwan), with real regulatory and democratic institutions. That way, as they plug into the global system they can handle its inevitable surges and excesses. The real crisis will come if we don't take advantage of this moment.

We want to keep global capital flows as free as possible—and even if we didn't, there's no way to restrict them anymore.

All sorts of would-be geo-architects want to set up some new global institutions to slow down capital flows. This is both wrong and futile. We want to keep global capital flows as free as possible—and even if we didn't, there's no way to restrict them anymore. The answer for countries is local, not global.

I like to compare countries to computers. Today, for the first time in history, we all have the same basic piece of hardware—free markets. The question is, which countries will get the economic operating systems (neoliberal macroeconomics) and software (regulatory institutions and laws) to get the most out of those free markets and cushion them from the worst surges coming from the "electronic herd" of global investors.

Russia is the egregious example of a country that plugged into the herd with no operating system and no software, with predictably horrendous results. Thailand, South Korea and Indonesia plugged into the herd, but with a slow operating system: what I call "DOS-capital 2.0" (crony capitalism). It was great for getting these countries from an average income of $500 per capita to $5,000. But when they wanted to move from $5,000 to $15,000, and the speed of the electronic herd moved from a 286 chip to a Pentium III, and they were still using DOScapital 2.0, a message came up on their screens: "You Have Performed a Series of Irrational Investments. Cannot Save Items. Delete Memory of All Inefficient Banks and Firms, and Download New Software and Operating System."

As President Ernesto Zedillo of Mexico once remarked to me, at the end of the day every global dollar invested in Mexico ends up in a "local" Mexican bank, a "local" Mexican insurance company, a "local" Mexican factory. If Mexico does not have the operating system and rule-of-law software to manage and regulate that dollar, he said, no global institution can save it.

Bad lenders can be just as dangerous as bad borrowers, and some of the worst lenders in recent years have been big banks. A friend of mine in Hong Kong said that during the Asian economic boom, Germany's Dresdner Bank told its managers in Asia, "Lend, lend, lend, otherwise we will lose market share." Banks make money by lending and each one assumed that Asia was a no-brainer. So they shoved money out the door, just like drug dealers expanding their client base. Their message to the developing world was: "C'mon kid. Just try a little of this cash. The first loan's free."

Another form of bad lending is when banks recklessly lend millions of dollars to hedge funds so that they can "leverage" their bets. The hedge funds raise $1 from investors, borrow $9 more from banks and then use that leverage to magnify each of their bets in stocks, bonds, derivatives and currencies around the world. Generally speaking, there is nothing wrong with leverage. Your home mortgage is leverage. You want people to take risks, even crazy risks. This is how fledgling enterprises get financed and either go bankrupt or turn into Microsoft. The danger with leverage derives from the fact that the amounts of money that can be lent to hedge funds or emerging markets today are so enormous, and the system is now so greased and integrated, that when big risk-takers like Long-Term Capital Management make big mistakes they can destabilize everyone.

Right now, our understanding of the globalization system is about as sophisticated as our understanding of the cold-war system was in 1946.

How to reduce that threat? To begin with, we need to proceed slowly and humbly. By this I mean that we have to understand that the global economic system is still so new and so fast that even the best minds don't fully understand how it works. Right now, our understanding of the globalization system is about as sophisticated as our understanding of the cold-war system was in 1946. Alan Greenspan is a lifelong scholar of international finance. But when I asked him in December about the logic of today's integrated global market, he gave me a rare on-the-record quote that should humble us all. "I have learned more about how this new international financial system works in the last 12 months," he said, "than in the previous 20 years."

Some have proposed that we put a little sand in the gears of the global economy to slow it down a bit. My response would be that I don't think it is ever very wise to put sand in the gears of a machine when you don't fully understand how it works. It might not just slow down. It could come to a screeching, metal-bending halt. Also, where do you put the sand when you are dealing with a fund manager sitting in Connecticut using the Internet to invest in Brazil via a bank domiciled offshore in Panama? Ever try to put sand in cyberspace? Well, then, how about setting up a global central bank? That may be a good idea, but it's not something that is going to happen anytime soon—not as long as we all still live in 200-odd different countries.

So does that mean that there is nothing we can do? No. The good news is that in the wake of the crisis of 1998-99 the market on its own is brutally disciplining itself. You see signs of this everywhere.

Global financial crises will be the norm in the coming era.

The chief executives of some of the biggest banks in the world—Barclays P.L.C., BankAmerica, United Bank of Switzerland—were all ousted in 1998, after huge losses in high-risk emerging markets.

In the wake of these beheadings, those major banks have restricted leverage, cutting off reckless fund managers, demanding more documentation from those to whom they are still lending and scrutinizing more seriously not just the balance-of-payments figures of emerging markets but also their operating systems, legal systems and overall software.

Banks and investors have started asking fund managers tough questions about their exposure to risks and what defensive measures they have taken. And the International Monetary Fund, the Treasury and fund managers have belatedly started asking emerging-market countries what they are doing to improve their financial and regulatory systems.

The only realistic solution for now is to take this ad hoc approach, intensify it and extend it into the future. If everyone from the I.M.F. to Merrill Lynch to my Aunt Bev would just ask these questions more often, and keep asking them, we'd have a chance of preventing two out of the next five crises and limiting the impact of one of the next five. That's the most we can hope for.

Sure, this doesn't seem very sexy—calling on everyone in the system to become a better regulator, a smarter investor and a more prudent lender. But it's time we stopped kidding ourselves. Today's markets are so big and, with the advent of the Internet, becoming so fast that they can never be immunized from crises.

Global financial crises will be the norm in the coming era. In fact, let me leave you, dear readers, with one piece of advice: Fasten your seat belts and put your seat backs and tray tables into a fixed and upright position. Because the booms and the busts and the recoveries will all be coming faster. So get used to it, and just try to make sure that the leverage in the system doesn't become so great in any one area that it can make the whole system go boom or bust. Anyone who tells you that they have a plan for eliminating these crises is just pulling your leg. In fact, as you are reading these words, the next global financial crisis is already germinating somewhere.

Geopolitics

It is not easy for this generation of Americans to grasp how important the United States is to the world in the era of globalization. America today is the Michael Jordan of geopolitics—the overwhelmingly dominant system. Now Jordan was good, and his opponents both loved and hated playing against him. Everyone wanted to be like Mike. But as good as Jordan was, he was nothing without all the other teams in the N.B.A. to showcase his skills—and we're nothing without the rest of the world, which is why managing globalization is a role from which America dare not shrink.

> *America today is the Michael Jordan of geopolitics— the overwhelmingly dominant system.*

Historically, the United States has either been isolated from world affairs or deeply engaged as part of a moral crusade to fend off an aggressive, threatening power. Isolation is easy to explain and understand. Engagement in a bipolar world—with a menacing, nuclear-armed Soviet bear growling on the other side— was easy to explain and understand. But what is not easy to explain or understand is engagement in a world in which America is the biggest beneficiary and the sole superpower, with multiple secondary powers and no immediately visible threat, but with many little threats and an abstract globalization system to maintain. But this is the world we have. And in this world we can't afford either to retreat into isolation or to wait around for some smaller adversary to become a life-threatening foe.

As I have noted before, globalization and economic integration will act, to some degree, as a restraint on those states that are plugged into the system and dependent upon the electronic herd. It's true that no two countries that both have a McDonald's have ever fought a war since they each got their McDonald's. (I call this the Golden Arches Theory of Conflict Prevention.) But globalization does not end geopolitics—the enduring quest for power, the fear of neighbors, the tug of history. What globalization does is simply put a different frame around geopolitics, a frame that raises the costs of war but cannot eliminate it.

That is why sustainable globalization still requires a stable, geopolitical power structure, which simply cannot be maintained without the active involvement of the United States. All the technologies that Silicon Valley is designing to carry digital voices, videos and data around the world, all the trade and financial integration it is promoting through its innovations and all the wealth this is generating, are happening in a world stabilized by a benign superpower, with its capital in Washington, D.C.

The hidden hand of the market will never work without a hidden fist—McDonald's cannot flourish without McDonnell Douglas, the builder of the F-15. And the hidden fist that keeps the world safe for Silicon Valley's technologies is called the United States Army, Air Force, Navy and Marine Corps. "Good ideas and technologies need a strong power that promotes those ideas by example and protects those ideas by winning on the battlefield," says the foreign policy historian Robert Kagan. "If a lesser power were promoting our ideas and technologies, they would not have the global currency that they have. And when a strong power, the Soviet Union, promoted its bad ideas, they had a lot of currency for more than half a century."

This is too easily forgotten today. For too many executives in Silicon Valley, there is no geography or geopolitics anymore. There are only stock options and electrons. Their view that Washington is the enemy, and that any tax dollar paid there is a tax dollar wasted, is grotesque. There is a saying in Silicon Valley that "loyalty is just one mouse-click away." But you can take that too far. Execs there make boasts like: "We are not an American company. We are I.B.M. U.S., I.B.M. Canada, I.B.M. Australia, I.B.M. China." Oh, yeah? Then, the next time I.B.M. China gets in trouble in China, call Jiang Zemin for help. And the next time Congress closes another military base in Asia, call Microsoft's navy to secure the sea lanes of the Pacific. And the next time Congress wants to close more consulates and embassies, call Amazon.com to order a new passport.

This doesn't mean America needs to be involved everywhere all the time. There are big, important places and there are small, unimportant places. Diplomacy is about knowing the difference between the two, and knowing how to mobilize others to act where we cannot or should not act alone.

In such a world, pure realism and pure idealism are rarely the answer. The realists would say, Stay away from Kosovo, even if the conflict could spill over to Greece and Turkey; the idealists argue that we should invade Serbia with NATO forces, break off Kosovo, make it an independent state and defend it forever. Both are wrong.

The lesson I learned from Bosnia is that Americans do not want to watch innocent civilians slaughtered in Europe, especially when we have the resources to make a difference at a reasonable cost. And they are right. But those who argued that no NATO peacekeeping operation would be workable in Bosnia until the parties were exhausted and there was a balance of power on the ground were also right. When you talk to American troops and officers who have served in Bosnia as peacekeepers, they don't tell you that they feel stuck in some morass. They are genuinely proud of what they are doing and vastly prefer that to parading around the flagpole at Fort Hood.

In Kosovo, the instinct of the Clinton Administration to nudge the parties toward a settlement before another massacre, and to leverage American power—sending 4,000 peacekeepers to the Europeans' 25,000—basically makes sense. If the parties in Kosovo are ready to make peace, America, as a European power, should be prepared to play a part in patrolling the fence between them. If they are not, we should build a fence around them and use our leverage to foster a balance of power.

This same delicate balance applies to China. America's China policy oscillates between the Boeing School (just do business and everything will take care of itself) and the neoconservative school (China is a new version of the old Soviet Union and must be contained). Both are wrong. We do not want a cold war with China if we can avoid it.

China is not the Soviet Union, which made television sets that blew up and tractors that were more valuable as scrap metal. China is one-fifth of humanity and an economic powerhouse. It is also changing profoundly because of its openness to the world, and anyone who visits there regularly can see that it's Madison, not Mao, who's winning the day there. The right approach to China is to build bridges where possible—to nurture that openness—and draw redlines where necessary when Chinese actions become destabilizing. And some days you have to draw redlines in the morning and build bridges in the afternoon. We get in trouble when we do only one and not the other.

The right approach to China is to build bridges where possible . . . and draw redlines where necessary when Chinese actions become destabilizing.

In order to sustain such policies, proponents of internationalism are going to have to build a new coalition to support it. The constituency that sustained internationalism for 50 years was the so-called Eastern Intellectual Establishment. That establishment, to the extent it even exists today, doesn't carry much weight with the I'm-an-idiot-and-proud-of-it Congressmen, who boast that they never travel abroad and, in some cases, don't even hold passports.

The next Administration, whether Democratic or Republican, will have to try to bring together the new globalizers—from software writers to Web-page designers, from Iowa farmers to environmental activists, from human rights campaigners to high-tech assembly-line workers—to form a new, 21st-century coalition that can sustain internationalism. This new coalition doesn't exist yet, so someone is going to have to put it together.

This won't be easy. Americans were ready to pay any price and bear any burden in the cold war because there was a compelling and immediate sense that their own homes and way of life were threatened. But a large majority don't feel that way about North Korea, Iraq or Kosovo, and while Russia may still have the capability to pose a lethal threat, it is not doing so at this time. That's why Americans are in the odd position now of being held responsible for everything, while being reluctant to die for anything. That's why in the globalization era, counterinsurgency is out; baby-sitting is in. House-to-house fighting is out; cruise missiles are in. Green Berets are out; U.N. blue helmets are in.

America truly is the ultimate benign superpower and reluctant enforcer. But history teaches us that if you take this reluctance too far, you can undermine the whole system. Paul Schroeder, emeritus professor of international history at the University of Illinois, is one of the great international historians of the 20th century. He once remarked to me: "If you look at history, the periods of relative peace are those in which there is a durable, stable and tolerable hegemon, who does the adjusting and preserves the minimal necessary norms and rules of the game. And that hegemony always pays a disproportionate share of the collective costs, even forgoes opportunities for conquest or restrains itself in other ways, so as not to build up resentments and to make sure the system stays tolerable for others.

"The difficulty," Schroeder continued, "comes when the benign hegemonic power, which is responsible for keeping the system stable, is unable or unwilling to pay the disproportionate costs to do so, or its hegemony becomes intolerable and predatory rather than benign, or when enough actors rebel against its rules and insist upon a different kind of system that may not benefit that hegemony."

Too Many Flags?[2]

By Juan Enriquez
Foreign Policy, Fall 1999

During the last half of the twentieth century, there has been a trend toward more and smaller states. Three-quarters of the flags woven into military uniforms, painted on planes, and saluted in classrooms throughout the world today did not exist 50 years ago. As the number of sovereign states in the United Nations has increased from 51 to 185 (soon to be 187), the rate of new-country creation has varied. From 1950 to 1990, 2.2 new states were created per year, up from an average of 1.2 per year from 1900 to 1950. The 1990s have seen extreme instability: From 1990 to 1998, the rate was 3.1 new countries per year.

Throughout history, the dissolution of countries has been primarily a consequence of wars between states. Today, governments have more to fear from within than without. In Africa, Asia, Europe, and the former Soviet Union, major external wars and disputes over border regions are taking a back seat to internal challenges. Groups within the state are asserting their ethnic, religious, linguistic, regional, or national identities and questioning the integrity and legitimacy of existing countries. Internal turmoil increasingly leads to abrupt border changes.

The spectacle of civil strife in the developing world and within the former communist bloc has engendered the stereotype that only weak and underdeveloped countries produce new states. This assumption is wrong. Having an educated population, a strong regional economy, a democracy, a shared language, a common religion, or great cultural and historical achievements does not guarantee the success or survival of a particular state. In 1920, Europe had 23 states. By 1994, it had 44. Small European nations such as Belgium are now considering the benefits of granting more autonomy to provinces and regions, rather than having a strong central government. When one considers that Europe had approximately 500 political entities in 1500, it appears that the unwinding of the continent's existing countries could continue for a long time.

So far, the Western Hemisphere is the one segment of the world that has seemed immune from secessionist impulses. Although the Caribbean Basin has continued generating microstates, the last

---

new border to emerge in the Americas was Panama in 1903 and before that El Salvador in 1841. Except in Québec, questioning flags, borders, and anthems typically does not form part of the discourse of even the most radical leaders in the hemisphere. Guerrillas in Chiapas, Colombia, and Guatemala are not asking for separate states. In the United States, some of the most fervent advocates of "states" rights" are also the most ardent nationalists.

But boundaries within the Western Hemisphere are neither as simple nor as stable as they appear. As the U.S. flag grew from 13 to 50 stars (plus a number of territories), it kept parts of Canada, Denmark, England, France, Hawaii, Japan, Mexico, Russia, Samoa, and Spain. This expansion also gave birth to several states, including Cuba, Micronesia, Palau, and the Philippines. The U.S.-Mexican land border changed as recently as 1963, and the current maritime border was only approved by Congress in 1997. Newfoundland reluctantly left the United Kingdom to join Canada in 1949. Part of France's border, represented by St. Pierre and Miquelon, lies less than 15 miles off the Canadian coast. Québec may separate, perhaps leading to the dissolution of Canada.

In reality, globalization is breaking the world down into its component parts, even as it is drawing these parts closer together.

Despite such fluctuations, most leaders throughout the Americas rarely consider the possibility that their current borders may shrink or even disappear. This "it can't happen here" mentality rests on a false premise. Contrary to popular perception, the tide of secessionism that is sweeping across the world today is not simply a product of ancient nationalist impulses and catastrophic social unrest. It is also being driven, in part, by globalization, which leaves no country untouched.

Intuitively, one might expect globalization to bring countries together rather than tear them apart. The erosion of borders and changing notions of sovereignty are supposed to dampen nationalist desires, not inflame them. It holds less meaning, for example, to be a citizen of Germany now that the country's French neighbors are fellow citizens of the European Union (EU) who use the same currency and are guaranteed the same rights under the law. But in reality, globalization is breaking the world down into its component parts, even as it is drawing these parts closer together.

It Can Happen Here

Traditional explanations of why a state splits or disappears usually focus on historical cleavages along lines of religion, ethnicity, language, and culture. Another possible cause cited is the invasion or departure of a foreign power. These factors explain why, after centuries of ebb and flow, conflicts such as those in the former Yugoslavia are sometimes best understood by looking at maps that are centuries old. Likewise, future maps of Africa may mirror the continent's precolonial divisions more closely. As useful as such explanations may be, they tell only part of the story. Civil wars also occur in places where there are no clear religious or ethnic divisions, as happened in China, Russia, Spain, and the United States. Furthermore, historical divisions do not allow one to predict when a state might split.

Just as Spain and the United Kingdom are fraying apart after centuries as unified nation-states, so too are their American offspring now subject to the tug of new centrifugal forces along their borders. Secession is not only a less traumatic process, but it may also lead to greater prosperity for wealthy regions. The newfound respect for human rights and the spread of democracy have brought a plethora of previously repressed debates bubbling to the surface. The growing tendency to justify and base governance on the grounds of maintaining economic efficiency has opened the door to secessionists who can legitimately claim that they are not reaping the benefits of economic restructuring. Because dissolution often occurs within a nation's borders, using military force, whether local or foreign, to enforce the status quo is now more difficult and costly. Today, governments wishing to keep their borders intact must treat their citizens as if they were shareholders capable of selling their stock, forcing a change in management, or downsizing the state as if it were a business conglomerate. After all, a corporation is worth more than its individual parts. Similarly, in order to survive, the whole of a country has to be worth more than its individual regions.

The Diminishing Cost of Secession

The more globalized the world becomes, the less traumatic it is for nationalists to split from their states. Consider, for example, the Québecois, who for centuries have cherished and defended their language and culture. Driven by the perception that 25 million English Canadians are culturally overwhelming 5.7 million Francophones, they periodically try to separate from Canada. Given this fear of Anglo speech and thought, why is Québec the Canadian province most in favor of establishing a free-trade area with the United States? Why would the Québecois want open borders with 270 million additional English speakers? Globalization implies that borders become more porous to goods, ideas, capital, and people. If it is just as easy for Québec to trade north-south as it is east-west, Canada's market, not to mention its laws and rules, are no longer essential to the province's survival. In fact, small countries and national groups hoping to avoid domination by larger neighbors sometimes find open borders their best ally. This rationale explains why some European separatists, such as the Catalans and the Basques in Spain, also strongly support further integration within the EU.

Country disintegration is enabled by integration on a supranational level. States at once fragment and cluster. As a country's control within its own borders weakens, its influence abroad may increase. The Brazilian central government could not prevent the local governor of Minas Gerais from defaulting on payments owed to the country's treasury—a move that prompted a sudden devaluation and global financial jitters. Yet Brazil (and by extension Minas Gerais) reaps increasing influence and benefits from its influential role in MERCOSUR, the world's fastest-growing trade bloc. European integration allows Spain to be on a more equal footing with France and Germany. The same, however, holds true for Basque separatists. Twenty years ago, Basques had to carry Spanish passports and could work only in Spain. Today, they carry European passports and can work anywhere in the EU. [See table on page 27.] If the Basques chose to put up a border and establish a country, this decision would not lead to long customs lines, a new currency, or the loss of trade, work, or travel privileges. Autonomy would strengthen local governance. Without European integration, however, such autonomy would neither be profitable nor, perhaps, even feasible.

Size Doesn't Matter

Throughout history, countries have sought to expand. Starting with ancient Egypt and the Roman Empire and on to the European age of colonization, the name of the game seemed to be "more is better": more people, land, trees, gold, oil, or diamonds. Because the path to power often led countries through their neighbors' backyards, between 1820 and 1945 nine out of ten wars around the world involved border disputes. Pursuant to the doctrine of Manifest Destiny, which gave the United States the impetus to expand throughout the North American continent, U.S. territory grew to four-and-a-half times its original size by 1945.

Today, the goal of most wars is to make countries smaller rather than larger. One reason for this development is that most contemporary Goliath states are singularly unsuccessful. Consider, for example, Brazil, China, India, and Indonesia, where almost half of the world's inhabitants now live. Despite extraordinary human and nat-

The Basques as Europeans	
Twenty Years Ago	**Today**
Carried Spanish passport	Carries European Union (EU) passport
Traded under Spanish Customs Authority	Unified Market encompasses 15 European countries
Could only work in Spain	Can work anywhere in EU
Spanish government was responsible for security and foreign policy	Europe is evolving toward a common foreign and security policy
Regulators and bureaucrats were Spanish	More regulatory decisions are undertaken in Brussels by European institutions
Courts and legislators were Spanish	Spain increasingly intergrated within European legal system
Spanish was only language	EU has 11 official languages and Basque is spoken freely
Currency was paeseta	Currency will soon be exclusively Euro
Central bank was Spanish	Central bank is European
Trade agreements tended to be bilateral	Trade agreements are through EU

ural resources, none of these states has become a developed country, and all face massive internal challenges that could lead to splits within their borders sometime early in the next century. Likewise, Russia—a landmass 562 times larger than Belgium—exports half as much as Belgium and almost 29 times less per person.

Small countries are among the fastest-growing and most effective traders in the post-World War II era. Luxembourg, Singapore, and Switzerland may all be geographically isolated and have almost no natural resources, but according to a World Economic Forum report on global competitiveness, these small countries are almost twice as competitive in terms of quality of infrastructure, technology, and business management as Australia, Ireland, New Zealand, the United States, and the United Kingdom, four times more than Asia's manufacturing states, almost six times more than the EU, and seven times more than Latin American states.

Certain regions within large states not only may be viable as separate states but also may be far more productive when unbundled from their traditional borders. The residents of Bali province in Indonesia, frustrated at seeing their lucrative tourist revenue siphoned off by the central government in Jakarta, have begun discussing regional autonomy. Within the Americas, relatively wealthy areas, such as western Canada, northern Mexico, southern Brazil, and the coastal city of Guayaquil in Ecuador, have voices of dissent within their borders asking what benefit they derive from their national identities. This development has coincided with the end of import substitution industrialization and the opening of borders. Countries and regions now depend on global, not local, markets. In the 1990s, Costa Rica and Uruguay, two of the Western Hemisphere's smallest nations, have grown faster than the Latin American average.

A nation's success in the global economy is not determined by the quantity of its natural resources, but by the quality of its human resources. A country cannot hope to remain competitive without an educated, skilled work force. Israel is only about 20,000 square kilometers in size and has a population of just 5.7 million. But whereas Israel lacks the oil resources of some of its Arab neighbors, its population publishes ten times more scientific and technical articles per person than the closest runner up, the United States. Israel has been able to cope with the massive immigration from the Soviet Union—which from 1990 to 1996 was equivalent to roughly 13 percent of its population—because 40 percent of those arriving have been scientists, engineers, and academics. One day its high-tech industry could rival Silicon Valley's. In today's world, a government that controls a vast tract of territory may be less relevant than one that supports education and embraces a regulatory framework promoting innovation and investment.

If the key to prosperity is a citizenry with a high degree of education and entrepreneurship, some regions may decide that retaining ties to areas that are underdeveloped and prone to conflict is not a good long-term strategy. Those citizens who end up happiest after a state splits are often those who have been the most blessed, not the most oppressed. In a quest to separate itself from its conflictive partners and join the EU, one of the first two areas to separate from Yugoslavia was also one of the richest, Slovenia. Similarly, the Czechs put up little resistance when Slovakia declared independence. Although the Czech region was 40 percent smaller than Czechoslovakia and had about one-third fewer people, its income per person was 20 percent higher than Slovakia's. Italy's northern secessionist movement, Liga Toscana, is symptomatic of the tensions between the rich north and poor south. The two most aggressive separatist groups in Spain—the Basques and the Catalans—are among the richest of Spaniards. Many western Canadians would be happy to let Québec and the Maritime Provinces go off on their own. In 1990, Alaskans—many of whom were irate over having to share lucrative mineral, oil, and gas royalties with the U.S. federal government—elected a governor who campaigned on a secessionist platform. Northern Mexicans often blame their financial troubles on political incompetence in Mexico City and resent the increasing immigration to their region from poorer areas such as Oaxaca.

Democracy As a Double-Edged Sword

Questions that were once brutally suppressed under dictatorships—such as the rights of minorities or other groups to secede from the state—often lead to contentious debates within emerging democracies. Democratization sometimes brings groups within a society face to face with what one writer has dubbed the state's "founding crimes, its hidden injuries and divisions, [and] its unhealed wounds." Political reform does not implicitly guarantee peace, stability, or growth, much less the integrity of a particular state. Colombia, a country divided by ongoing civil conflict, is South America's longest-running democracy. Czechoslovakia and some Yugoslav states held elections before they tore themselves apart. The dissolution of the Soviet Union followed perestroika. Debate over the future of Wales and Scotland gained momentum after British prime minister Tony Blair supported separate legislatures.

Countries and regions now depend on global, not local, markets.

Over the past two decades, almost all of the Americas have evolved toward greater democracy and respect for human rights. One consequence is far more support for, and legitimacy accorded to, the rights of indigenous minorities. Some of the more than 550 sovereign nations of indigenous peoples that exist within the United States are demanding rights accorded to them by treaties that have not been respected for centuries. These demands can lead to curious discontinuities in terms of sovereignty and law. The International Whaling Commission has granted an exception that allows the Makah Tribe of Washington State to hunt whales, in recognition of a treaty that the tribe signed with the U.S. government in 1855. In 1993, the U.S. Congress and President Bill Clinton acknowledged the "100th anniversary of the illegal overthrow [of the Hawaiian monarch] . . . which resulted in the suppression of the inherent right to sovereignty of the Native Hawaiian people." Five years later, in observation of the 100th anniversary of the

U.S. annexation of Hawaii, the state's governor called upon Hawaiians and non-Hawaiians alike to "advance a plan for Hawaiian sovereignty." As the United States and other developed countries demand respect for the rights of minorities throughout the world, it is getting harder for them to ignore mounting legal challenges posed by indigenous groups within their own borders.

Within Latin America, many voices are questioning the status quo, including Mapuches in Chile, Mayans throughout Chiapas and Central America, and descendants of Incas in Peru and Ecuador. Each group is asking what benefits it gets from belonging to a state that does not deliver what it promises. None of these movements begins or matures by advocating the splitting of the country or the rejection of flag and anthem. But redressing old grievances or contemporary needs, if mishandled, can eventually lead to escalating demands for autonomy and even separation. Like couples who divorce after a long marriage, nations and regions sometimes decide they are simply not compatible.

> *Political reform does not implicitly guarantee peace, stability, or growth, much less the integrity of a particular state.*

In the long term, however, there is no stable alternative to democracy. Within a democracy, arguments against splitting a country can be heard and debated. Canada has had time to redress grievances, build ties, and foster a sense of shared purpose. The nation has a fighting chance to hold together, by addressing not just the concerns of the Québecois but also of the Inuit, who now govern a territory more than twice the size of France and will soon receive self-governing status in Québec. The United Kingdom may remain united precisely because, in contrast to its historical performance in Northern Ireland, it is now providing open forums to discuss past grievances. The same is not true of dictatorships. When a state starts to split within an authoritarian system, there is little warning and, often, little to be done unless rulers are willing to commit extreme abuses against their populations.

Abandoning the Ship of State

The old adage "my country right or wrong" is under siege. Over the past decade, technocrats and democrats have tried hard to dismantle and discredit old populist, socialist, and communist institutions and beliefs in favor of free markets, open elections, and a globalized economy. They have mostly succeeded, but an unintended consequence of this new-found sense of pragmatism has been the increasing erosion of religion, nationalism, and a common culture—the bonds that often formed the basis for state creation.

If a government communicates to its constituents that its fundamental raison d'être is to privatize, limit services, eliminate bureaucrats, and balance budgets, those areas and citizens that most benefit or suffer from globalization may question how the state helps them.

When those who are disenfranchised and insecure try to change things, they often find little recourse through the electoral system. This frustration can lead to a more radical, fundamentalist, or regional discourse, and eventually to new borders. The Zapatista rebellion in Chiapas initially capitalized on the sense of fatigue throughout the region with Mexico City's technocrats and their free market focus. Regional discourse, demands for autonomy, and protests are growing in the Ecuadorian and Guatemalan highlands as well as among Brazil's landless. In richer regions, where economic efficiency is the prevailing ideology, many feel they do not need, or trust, their central governments. Politicians in northern Mexico and São Paulo, Brazil, are increasingly vocal in their demands for local autonomy and fiscal control.

Like couples who divorce after a long marriage, nations and regions sometimes decide they are simply not compatible.

Despite the now familiar dictum that "the era of big government is over," statistical evidence suggests otherwise. In the United States—where increases in fiscal expenditures have been more moderate than in most other nations—as a percentage of gross domestic product, government spending grew from 9 percent in 1937 to 33 percent in 1996. Yet democratic governments find themselves in a "Catch-22" situation—the more they bow to the ever-increasing demands of the electorate and spend money on public goods and services, the more disgruntled the electorate becomes. Speculation abounds as to why this phenomenon occurs: Some theorists argue that the taxes required to finance public programs (even popular ones) ultimately inhibit economic growth and engender widespread frustration.

Whatever the reason, it is clear that people are dissatisfied. At the end of the 1990s, despite unprecedented prosperity, only 34 percent of U.S. citizens trust their government. President Bill Clinton's scandals are not the root cause. There has been a steady decline in trust since the 1960s. Canadian polls indicate a similar collapse in confidence. A pair of surveys of 11 European countries conducted in 1981 and 1990 revealed a decline in public trust in six countries, with mixed results in four others. A 1998 poll compared the approval ratings and popularity of President Clinton with those of 14 Latin American leaders within their own borders; the U.S. president had a higher rating than the local leader in 11 countries. Lack of trust increases demands for regional autonomy. "If the guys in the capital won't take care of us," the argument goes, "we shall take care of ourselves."

Where Have All the Gunboats Gone?

Through diplomatic and economic pressure, coups, or outright invasions, the United States has often been a strong supporter of existing borders throughout the world. Even as the United States supports Iraqi opposition groups, it opposes autonomy for the Kurd-

---

Despite the invasions of Grenada (1983), Panama (1989), and Haiti (1994), it is getting harder for the United States to police the Western Hemisphere.

---

ish north and Shiite south. While waging war against Yugoslavia, it has not favored full sovereignty for Kosovo. Despite ethnic strife in Africa, few U.S. policymakers have advocated redrawing the continent's colonial-era borders.

The United States' role as a guarantor of the status quo has been most visible in the Americas, where, under the auspices of the Monroe Doctrine, it has staged more than 75 military interventions since 1851. But despite the invasions of Grenada (1983), Panama (1989), and Haiti (1994), it is getting harder for the United States to police the Western Hemisphere. Traditional justifications, such as expanding one's territory, fighting off European imperialists, or opposing communism, are now largely defunct. Although the United States continues to mediate border disputes between sovereign states such as Peru and Ecuador, or India and Pakistan, it is another matter to resolve internal challenges to a border's integrity. Troops still occasionally march off, claiming to fight drugs, ensure democracy, protect human rights, or oust the corrupt. But many of these conflicts imply getting involved in complex internal disputes and local governance, while enduring far tougher media scrutiny back home.

Furthermore, foreign interventions are less appealing in an era when even the most underdeveloped country can sometimes inflict unacceptable military and financial costs on great powers. It would be hard to find conflicts where the balance of power and resources were more skewed than in the U.S. war with North Vietnam, the intervention in Somalia, or the Soviet battle against the Afghans. These conflicts pitted the greatest military machines in the world against three of its least developed societies. Yet, in each case, the poor and underdeveloped "won." Despite its interest in Mexico's stability, the United States is unlikely to send troops to fight against an indigenous uprising in Chiapas. The same is true of the de facto division of Colombia. Advice, training, and intelligence will continue to flow. After Israel and Egypt, Colombia is the third leading recipient of U.S. security assistance in the world. But it is harder and harder for the United States to intervene directly. As the willingness (and ability) to intervene erodes, so does one of the pillars of hemispheric border stability.

From Subjects to Shareholders

In Scotland, each family clan identifies itself through tartan quilts. There are definite lines, but they overlap and blend in complex patterns. Describing these patterns is hard. Identifying them by sight is easy. Sovereignty today looks more like a tartan quilt than like the series of single colored shapes we see on classic maps. Functions and jurisdictions overlap, each distinct, but each occupying parts of the same space. Although each border and state's sovereignty follows a recognizable pattern, each is different. The extent of control over their territory is not the same for the governments of China, Mexico, the Republic of Congo, or the United States. They may claim many similar sovereign functions, but each government exercises a different degree of control.

Ambiguous or shared sovereignty is not new. Many countries have dealt with it in different ways. The German-Danish dispute over the border of the Schleswig-Holstein region was resolved only after the local population was granted significant autonomy and the assurance that children could, at the request of their parents, attend Danish-speaking schools. The League of Nations granted Finland sovereignty over the Swedish-speaking Ålands, an archipelago made up of 6,500 islands, on the condition that the Ålanders retain complete cultural and political autonomy. This agreement included control over immigration and provisions that allowed the Ålanders to keep their own flag and postage stamps. Panama's Kuna Indians control who may enter their islands, regardless of citizenship. In Canada, members of religious groups such as the Hutterites and the Mennonites pay income taxes as groups, not as individuals, and are subject to different legal regimes regarding property and inheritance.

What is different today is the breadth and power of actors that share sovereignty over a specific territory. We are long past the point when, to quote a textbook definition, a state was "a closed, impermeable, and sovereign unit, completely separated from other states." It is not that sovereignty has eroded, but rather that it has grown and unbundled, shifting from federal rulers to territorial authorities and now toward individuals. This development implies that the basis for a state's continued existence and success no longer hinges on its control over a specific territory or its funding a large army but on the legitimacy of its rule, its economic performance, and its ability to reconcile diverse ethnic, religious, and national aspirations. The centuries of gradual myth building that accumulated behind some flags and anthems is absent in more than half of today's countries.

States with diverse national groups or extreme regional divisions will not necessarily split, but the trend is in this direction, particularly for those that cannot deliver economic and personal security. The Americas may not have generated many new states in the past century and a half, but this does not guarantee that new countries will fail to emerge in the near future. Worldwide trends argue otherwise. The nations that comprise the "new world" of the Western Hemisphere have long taken comfort in the absence of historical cleavages and catastrophic conflicts that have afflicted their "old world" progenitors. But in an era of globalization, the secessionist impulse knows no geographical boundaries.

At This Rate, We'll Be Global in Another Hundred Years[3]

By Nicholas D. Kristof
New York Times, May 23, 1999

If anything seems obvious today, it is that globalization is a new and powerful force that is erasing national borders and linking the world in an unprecedented web of trade and investments. As one tycoon put it: "The world is a city."

But that was Baron Carl Meyer von Rothschild, in 1875, reacting as stock markets tumbled all around the world, in unison, feeding off each other.

Perhaps the greatest myth about globalization is that it is new. By some measures, its peak occurred a century ago, making the 20th century memorable in economic history mostly for its retreat from globalization. In some respects, only now is the world economy becoming roughly as interlinked as it was more than a century ago.

"We're still not back to where we were 100 years ago," said Charles W. Calomiris, a professor of finance and economics at the Columbia University's Graduate School of Business.

Labor is less mobile than it was in the last century. In those days, passports were unnecessary and people could travel freely from one country to the next, to visit or to work.

That mobility led 60 million Europeans to move to the Americas or Australia or elsewhere, and it helped fill up the United States. In 1900, according to the census, 14 percent of the American population was foreign born, compared to 8 percent today.

It's not just labor. The 1860's and 1870's were a golden era for free trade, and goods moved easily across borders. As late as 1879 an astonishing 95 percent of Germany's imports were still free of duty. Low trade barriers led to an explosion of trade, so that American exports soared to 7 percent of the gross national product in the late 1800's; it is 8 percent today.

Even capital seems to be less mobile now than in the 19th century. A "capital mobility index" prepared by the International Monetary Fund for a report in 1997 suggests that capital movements as a proportion of economic output are still well below the levels of the 1880's.

How can this be? A century ago, England and France invested hugely in developing countries—places like the United States, Australia and Canada. England invested a larger share of its wealth abroad at that time than it does now.

Foreign capital financed one-third of domestic investment in New Zealand and Canada in the late 19th century, and one-quarter in Sweden. In contrast, foreign capital accounted for only about 10 percent of domestic investment in emerging markets in the 1990's, according to the I.M.F.

"To me as an economic historian, it was really the 19th century that represented the birth of the global economy," said Alan M. Taylor, an economist at Northwestern University. "These days, it's just getting back to where it was 100 years ago."

> *In some respects, globalization predates the 19th century.*

Mr. Taylor suggested that 19th-century investors might well have had a larger share of their stock portfolios invested abroad than investors do today. He noted that Americans often have living rooms full of goods from all over the world, but their portfolios still tend to be focused in the United States. That discrepancy, he said, may be an anachronism related to financial markets being less globalized than markets for goods (at least until recently).

In some respects, globalization predates the 19th century. Chinese demand for silver in the 16th through 18th centuries played a role in financing the Spanish empire and the slave trade. China absorbed perhaps half of the global production of silver, and that bolstered prices and created wealth for mining magnates in the Americas—who traded their silver for slaves. After passing through several hands, the silver was used to purchase Chinese porcelain and silk.

Although it is often said today that globalization is irreversible, it proved very reversible early in this century. After economic integration reached a peak in the late 19th century, there was an astonishing retreat after World War I and especially after the Great Depression. Since World War II, trade and international investment rose again, and they have soared in the last couple of decades.

"After the first world war, we had a massive interruption and reversal of the long-term trend," said Jagdish Bhagwati, an international economist at Columbia University. "One interpretation is that now we're just climbing back on that trend."

Still, today's globalization is new in some important ways, and arguably it touches many more people than the earlier kind. Professor Bhagwati noted that trade in the 19th century consisted mostly of commodities. Now it is mainly manufactured goods with parts from so many countries that it is difficult to describe the finished products as made in any one nation.

Capital flows are also different, says David Hale, chief global economist of the Zurich Group, a financial services company. In the 19th century, capital movements represented the savings of a relatively small group of prosperous families in England and France who were investing for the long term. Today investments are far more broadly based, he said, and much more likely to be leveraged and short term, more flighty and speculative.

One result is that capital rushes around the globe much more quickly than ever before, and is more prone to sweep into countries and then out. Technology has created an electronic herd but as yet no electronic cowboys to control the herd.

Indeed, for a world without telephones or computers, the 19th century had its economic advantages. Output shot up and down like a roller coaster, but mostly up. Professor Calomiris has recorded 90 major banking crises over the last 20 years, and he notes that they often led to runs on national currencies. In contrast, in the period from 1870 to 1913, he can find only five major banking crises, and just one of those led to an exchange rate crisis. In many ways, he argues, 19th-century globalization worked better than today's.

"It's very hard to recapture the successes of the earlier period," Professor Calomiris said, but he thinks it is worth a try. It may seem heretical to tinker with the 21st-century process by looking over one's shoulder for models a hundred years past, but it is a reminder that globalization may well be older than nationalization.

II. Show Me the Money: Business and the Global Economy

Editor's Introduction

When people speak of globalization, they often mean the economy, particularly those parts dealing with trade, investment, and companies. With the breaking down of trade barriers and the spread of open markets (when no protective tarriffs or taxes are attached to goods), it has become easier, and cheaper, to buy products from around the world. Large companies, once monoliths only in their own lands, have expanded their realm to include satellites in other countries and are now designated as TNCs (transnational companies) or MNCs (multinational companies). Economic factors probably dominate discussions of globalization because businesses and their mega-merger deals are so visible. As the saying goes, money makes the world go round.

Our era is certainly not the first to trade on the global level. We need look no further than the empires of the 19th century to find heavy exchanges of raw material (from the colonies) and manufactured goods (from the protectorate nations). There are, however, certain factors in existence today that foster an environment in which global trade is easy and, some think, beneficial. Technology, in particular the birth of the Internet and the World Wide Web, and advances in telecommunications have shrunk the world and allowed for quick dissemination of information. Business managers have adjusted to this new level of communications by transferring operations, sometimes even management services, to places that once seemed too remote. From the other direction, citizens of so-called third-world nations began to migrate to richer countries, searching for better pay and conditions. In the "The Nanny Chain" (from *American Prospect*), Arlie Russell Hochschild points out that women are migrating in ever greater numbers. She focuses on the "global care chain," a shift of caregivers as women move to work in richer nations, leaving their children to be cared for by older daughters or girls who hail from even poorer nations.

As companies learned to accomodate new labor forces, they needed to adjust to new markets as well. For example, when McDonalds opened a restaurant outside of the United States, managers found that certain practices would not work because of cultural differences. In "China's Big Mac Attack" (from *Foreign Affairs*), James L. Watson asserts that McDonalds is now so much a part of Chinese life that many Chinese citizens (especially those in urban areas with long-time McDonalds restaurants nearby) regard the chain as indigenous. It did not start out that way of course. Just as McDonalds' culture influenced China, Chinese culture altered the practices and mentality of its McDonalds restaurants.

In the third article, "Customizing the World on the Web" (from *Information Today*), Robin Peek explores how local customs and laws will affect how we do business on the Internet. Since the world is unlikely to agree on "contentious issues," she recommends that companies start to customize their content and their operations for foreign markets.

Peek's observation that people are not going to agree any time soon is seconded by Sarah Anderson and John Cavanagh, who wrote an article with Thea Lee entitled "We Can Fight, We Can Win" for the *Nation*. Noting that large, faceless TNCs and MNCs often conduct business as if they have no restrictions (including ethics), the authors argue that citizens can change the course of business. By contrast, Bruce Stokes, in "The Protectionist Myth" (from *Foreign Policy*), cautions against too much backlash. He distinguishes between "old" protectionism ("efforts to protect the narrow economic interests of one industry at the expense of another") and "new" protectionism ("efforts to use trade sanctions to enforce labor, environmental, and health standards"). He asserts that globalization is reversible, if we so wish it, but it is also a positive trend and should be encouraged for the most part.

The Nanny Chain[1]

BY ARLIE RUSSELL HOCHSCHILD
AMERICAN PROSPECT, JANUARY 3, 2000

Vicky Diaz, a 34-year-old mother of five, was a college-educated schoolteacher and travel agent in the Philippines before migrating to the United States to work as a housekeeper for a wealthy Beverly Hills family and as a nanny for their two-year-old son. Her children, Vicky explained to Rhacel Parrenas, "were saddened by my departure. Even until now my children are trying to convince me to go home. The children were not angry when I left because they were still very young when I left them. My husband could not get angry either because he knew that was the only way I could seriously help him raise our children, so that our children could be sent to school. I send them money every month."

In her forthcoming book *Servants of Globalization,* Parrenas, an affiliate of the Center for Working Families at the University of California, Berkeley, tells an important and disquieting story of what she calls the "globalization of mothering." The Beverly Hills family pays "Vicky" (which is the pseudonym Parrenas gave her) $400 a week, and Vicky, in turn, pays her own family's live-in domestic worker back in the Philippines $40 a week. Living like this is not easy on Vicky and her family. "Even though it's paid well, you are sinking in the amount of your work. Even while you are ironing the clothes, they can still call you to the kitchen to wash the plates. It . . . [is] also very depressing. The only thing you can do is give all your love to [the two-year-old American child]. In my absence from my children, the most I could do with my situation is give all my love to that child."

Vicky is part of what we could call a global care chain: a series of personal links between people across the globe based on the paid or unpaid work of caring. A typical global care chain might work something like this: An older daughter from a poor family in a third world country cares for her siblings (the first link in the chain) while her mother works as a nanny caring for the children of a nanny migrating to a first world country (the second link) who, in turn, cares for the child of a family in a rich country (the final link). Each kind of chain expresses an invisible human ecology of care, one care worker depending on another and so on. A global

---

care chain might start in a poor country and end in a rich one, or it might link rural and urban areas within the same poor country. More complex versions start in one poor country and extend to another slightly less poor country and then link to a rich country.

Global care chains may be proliferating. According to 1994 estimates by the International Organization for Migration, 120 million people migrated—legally or illegally—from one country to another. That's 2 percent of the world's population. How many migrants leave loved ones behind to care for other people's children or elderly parents, we don't know. But we do know that more than half of legal migrants to the United States are women, mostly between ages 25 and 34. And migration experts tell us that the proportion of women among migrants is likely to rise. All of this suggests that the trend toward global care chains will continue.

How are we to understand the impact of globalization on care? If, as globalization continues, more global care chains form, will they be "good" care chains or "bad" ones? Given the entrenched problem of third world poverty—which is one of the starting points for care chains—this is by no means a simple question. But we have yet to fully address it, I believe, because the world is globalizing faster than our minds or hearts are. We live global but still think and feel local.

> *If, as globalization continues, more global care chains form, will they be "good" care chains or "bad" ones?*

Freud in a Global Economy

Most writing on globalization focuses on money, markets, and labor flows, while giving scant attention to women, children, and the care of one for the other. Most research on women and development, meanwhile, draws a connection between, say, World Bank loan conditions and the scarcity of food for women and children in the third world, without saying much about resources expended on caregiving. Much of the research on women in the United States and Europe focuses on a chainless, two-person picture of "work-family balance" without considering the child care worker and the emotional ecology of which he or she is a part. Fortunately, in recent years, scholars such as Ernestine Avila, Evelyn Nakano Glenn, Pierette Hondagneu-Sotelo, Mary Romero, and Rhacel Parrenas have produced some fascinating research on domestic workers. Building on this work, we can begin to focus on the first world end of the care chain and begin spelling out some of the implications of the globalization of love.

One difficulty in understanding these implications is that the language of economics does not translate easily into the language of psychology. How are we to understand a "transfer" of feeling from one link in a chain to another? Feeling is not a "resource" that can be crassly taken from one person and given to another. And surely one person can love quite a few people; love is not a resource limited the same way oil or currency supply is. Or is it?

Consider Sigmund Freud's theory of displacement, the idea that emotion can be redirected from one person or object to another. Freud believed that if, for example, Jane loves Dick but Dick is emotionally or literally unavailable, Jane will find a new object (say, John, Dick and Jane's son) onto which to project her original feeling for Dick. While Freud applied the idea of displacement mainly to relations within the nuclear family, the concept can also be applied to relations extending far outside it. For example, immigrant nannies and au pairs often divert feelings originally directed toward their own children toward their young charges in this country. As Sau-ling C. Wong, a researcher at the University of California, Berkeley, has put it, "Time and energy available for mothers are diverted from those who, by kinship or communal ties, are their more rightful recipients."

If it is true that attention, solicitude, and love itself can be "displaced" from one child (let's say Vicky Diaz's son Alfredo, back in the Philippines) onto another child (let's say Tommy, the son of her employers in Beverly Hills), then the important observation to make here is that this displacement is often upward in wealth and power. This, in turn, raises the question of the equitable distribution of care. It makes us wonder, is there—in the realm of love—an analogue to what Marx calls "surplus value," something skimmed off from the poor for the benefit of the rich?

Seen as a thing in itself, Vicky's love for the Beverly Hills toddler is unique, individual, private. But might there not be elements in this love that are borrowed, so to speak, from somewhere and someone else? Is time spent with the first world child in some sense "taken" from a child further down the care chain? Is the Beverly Hills child getting "surplus" love, the way immigrant farm workers give us surplus labor? Are first world countries such as the United States importing maternal love as they have imported copper, zinc, gold, and other ores from third world countries in the past?

This is a startling idea and an unwelcome one, both for Vicky Diaz, who needs the money from a first world job, and for her well-meaning employers, who want someone to give loving care to their child. Each link in the chain feels she is doing the right thing for good reasons—and who is to say she is not?

But there are clearly hidden costs here, costs that tend to get passed down along the chain. One nanny reported such a cost when she described (to Rhacel Parrenas) a return visit to the Philippines: "When I saw my children, I thought, 'Oh children do grow up even without their mother.' I left my youngest when she was only five years old. She was already nine when I saw her again but she still wanted for me to carry her [weeps]. That hurt me because it showed me that my children missed out on a lot."

Sometimes the toll it takes on the domestic worker is overwhelming and suggests that the nanny has not displaced her love onto an employer's child but rather has continued to long intensely for her own child. As one woman told Parrenas, "The first two years I felt like I was going crazy. . . . I would catch myself gazing at nothing, thinking about my child. Every moment, every second of the day, I felt like I was thinking about my baby. My youngest, you have to understand, I left when he was only two months old. . . . You know, whenever I receive a letter from my children, I cannot sleep. I cry. It's good that my job is more demanding at night."

Despite the anguish these separations clearly cause, Filipina women continue to leave for jobs abroad. Since the early 1990s, 55 percent of migrants out of the Philippines have been women; next to electronic manufacturing, their remittances make up the major source of foreign currency in the Philippines. The rate of female emigration has continued to increase and includes college-educated teachers, businesswomen, and secretaries. In Parrenas's study, more than half of the nannies she interviewed had college degrees and most were married mothers in their 30s.

Where are men in this picture? For the most part, men—especially men at the top of the class ladder—leave child-rearing to women. Many of the husbands and fathers of Parrenas's domestic workers had migrated to the Arabian peninsula and other places in search of better wages, relieving other men of "male work" as construction workers and tradesmen, while being replaced themselves at home. Others remained at home, responsible fathers caring or helping to care for their children. But some of the men tyrannized their wives. Indeed, many of the women migrants Parrenas interviewed didn't just leave; they fled. As one migrant maid explained:

> You have to understand that my problems were very heavy before I left the Philippines. My husband was abusive. I couldn't even think about my children, the only thing I could think about was the opportunity to escape my situation. If my husband was not going to kill me, I was probably going to kill him. . . . He always beat me up and my parents wanted me to leave him for a long time. I left my children with my sister. . . . In the plane. . . I felt like a bird whose cage had been locked for many years. . . . I felt free. . . Deep inside, I felt homesick for my children but I also felt free for being able to escape the most dire problem that was slowly killing me.

Other men abandoned their wives. A former public school teacher back in the Philippines confided to Parrenas: "After three years of marriage, my husband left me for another woman. My husband supported us for just a little over a year. Then the support was stopped. . . . The letters stopped. I have not seen him since." In the absence of government aid, then, migration becomes a way of coping with abandonment.

Sometimes the husband of a female migrant worker is himself a migrant worker who takes turns with his wife migrating. One Filipino man worked in Saudi Arabia for 10 years, coming home for a month each year. When he finally returned home for good, his wife set off to work as a maid in America while he took care of the children. As she explained to Parrenas, "My children were very sad when I left them. My husband told me that when they came back home from the airport, my children could not touch their food and they wanted to cry. My son, whenever he writes me, always draws the head of Fido the dog with tears on the eyes. Whenever he goes to Mass on Sundays, he tells me that he misses me more because he sees his friends with their mothers. Then he comes home and cries."

The End of the Chain

Just as global capitalism helps create a third world supply of mothering, it creates a first world demand for it.

Just as global capitalism helps create a third world supply of mothering, it creates a first world demand for it. The past half-century has witnessed a huge rise in the number of women in paid work—from 15 percent of mothers of children aged 6 and under in 1950 to 65 percent today. Indeed, American women now make up 45 percent of the American labor force. Three-quarters of mothers of children 18 and under now work, as do 65 percent of mothers of children 6 and under. In addition, a recent report by the International Labor Organization reveals that the average number of hours of work per week has been rising in this country.

Earlier generations of American working women would rely on grandmothers and other female kin to help look after their children; now the grandmothers and aunts are themselves busy doing paid work outside the home. Statistics show that over the past 30 years a decreasing number of families have relied on relatives to care for their children—and hence are compelled to look for nonfamily care. At the first world end of care chains, working parents are grateful to find a good nanny or child care provider, and they are generally able to pay far more than the nanny could earn in her native country. This is not just a child care problem. Many American families are now relying on immigrant or out-of-home care for their elderly relatives. As a Los Angeles elder-care worker, an immigrant, told Parrenas, "Domestics here are able to make a living from the elderly that families abandon." But this often means that nannies cannot take care of their own ailing parents and therefore produce an elder-care version of a child care chain—caring for first world elderly persons while a paid worker cares for their aged mother back in the Philippines.

My own research for two books, *The Second Shift* and *The Time Bind,* sheds some light on the first world end of the chain. Many women have joined the law, academia, medicine, business—but such professions are still organized for men who are free of family responsibilities. The successful career, at least for those who are broadly middle class or above, is still largely built on some key traditional components: doing professional work, competing with fellow professionals, getting credit for work, building a reputation while you're young, hoarding scarce time, and minimizing family obligations by finding someone else to deal with domestic chores. In the past, the professional was a man and the "someone else to deal with [chores]" was a wife. The wife oversaw the family, which—in pre-industrial times, anyway—was supposed to absorb the human vicissitudes of birth, sickness, and death that the workplace discarded. Today, men take on much more of the child care and housework at home, but they still base their identity on demanding careers in the context of which children are beloved impediments; hence, men resist sharing care equally at home. So when parents don't have enough "caring time" between them, they feel forced to look for that care further down the global chain.

The ultimate beneficiaries of these various care changes might actually be large multinational companies, usually based in the United States. In my research on a Fortune 500 manufacturing company I call Amerco, I discovered a disproportionate number of women employed in the human side of the company: public relations, marketing, human resources. In all sectors of the company, women often helped others sort out problems—both personal and professional—at work. It was often the welcoming voice and "soft touch" of women workers that made Amerco seem like a family to other workers. In other words, it appears that these working mothers displace some of their emotional labor from their children to their employer, which holds itself out to the worker as a "family." So, the care in the chain may begin with that which a rural third world mother gives (as a nanny) the urban child she cares for, and it may end with the care a working mother gives her employees as the vice president of publicity at your company.

How Much Is Care Worth?

How are we to respond to the growing number of global care chains? Through what perspective should we view them?

I can think of three vantage points from which to see care chains: that of the primordialist, the sunshine modernist, and (my own) the critical modernist. The primordialist believes that our primary responsibility is to our own family, our own community, our own country. According to this view, if we all tend our own primordial plots, everybody will be fine. There is some logic to this point of view. After all, Freud's concept of displacement rests on the premise that some original first object of love has a primary "right" to that love, and second and third comers don't fully share that right. (For the primordialist—as for most all of us—those first objects are members of one's most immediate family.) But the primordialist is an isolationist, an antiglobalist. To such a person, care chains seem wrong—not because they're unfair to the least-cared-for children at the bottom of the chain, but because they are global. Also, because family care has historically been provided by women, primordialists often believe that women should stay home to provide this care.

The sunshine modernist, on the other hand, believes care chains are just fine, an inevitable part of globalization, which is itself uncritically accepted as good. The idea of displacement is hard for the sunshine modernists to grasp because in their equation—seen mainly in economic terms—the global market will sort out who has proper claims on a nanny's love. As long as the global supply of labor meets the global demand for it, the sunshine modernist believes, everything will be okay. If the primordialist thinks care chains are bad because they're global, the sunshine modernist thinks they're good for the very same reason. In either case, the issue of inequality of access to care disappears.

The critical modernist embraces modernity but with a global sense of ethics. When the critical modernist goes out to buy a pair of Nike shoes, she is concerned to learn how low the wage was and how long the hours were for the third world factory worker making the shoes. The critical modernist applies the same moral concern to care chains: The welfare of the Filipino child back home must be seen as some part, however small, of the total picture. The critical modernist sees globalization as a very mixed blessing, bringing with it new opportunities—such as the nanny's access to good wages—but also new problems, including emotional and psychological costs we have hardly begun to understand.

From the critical modernist perspective, globalization may be increasing inequities not simply in access to money—and those inequities are important enough—but in access to care. The poor maid's child may be getting less motherly care than the first world child. (And for that matter, because of longer hours of work, the first world child may not be getting the ideal quantity of parenting attention for healthy development because too much of it is now displaced onto the employees of Fortune 500 companies.) We needn't lapse into primordialism to sense that something may be amiss in this.

I see no easy solutions to the human costs of global care chains. But here are some initial thoughts. We might, for example, reduce the incentive to migrate by addressing the causes of the migrant's economic desperation and fostering economic growth in the third world. Thus one obvious goal would be to develop the Filipino economy.

Sadly, the value ascribed to the labor of raising a child has always been low relative to the value of other kinds of labor, and under the impact of globalization, it has sunk lower still.

But it's not so simple. Immigration scholars have demonstrated that development itself can encourage migration because development gives rise to new economic uncertainties that families try to mitigate by seeking employment in the first world. If members of a family are laid off at home, a migrant's monthly remittance can see them through, often by making a capital outlay in a small business or paying for a child's education.

Other solutions might focus on individual links in the care chain. Because some women migrate to flee abusive husbands, a partial solution would be to create local refuges from such husbands. Another would be to alter immigration policy so as to encourage nannies to bring their children with them. Alternatively, employers or even government subsidies could help nannies make regular visits home.

The most fundamental approach to the problem is to raise the value of caring work and to ensure that whoever does it gets more credit and money for it. Otherwise, caring work will be what's left over, the work that's continually passed on down the chain. Sadly, the value ascribed to the labor of raising a child has always been low relative to the value of other kinds of labor, and under the impact of globalization, it has sunk lower still. The low value placed on caring work is due neither to an absence of demand for it (which is always high) nor to the simplicity of the work (successful caregiving is not easy) but rather to the cultural politics underlying this global exchange.

The declining value of child care anywhere in the world can be compared to the declining value of basic food crops relative to manufactured goods on the international market. Though clearly more essential to life, crops such as wheat, rice, or cocoa fetch low and declining prices while the prices of manufactured goods (relative to primary goods) continue to soar in the world market. And just as the low market price of primary produce keeps the third world low in the community of nations, the low market value of care keeps low the status of the women who do it.

One way to solve this problem is to get fathers to contribute more child care. If fathers worldwide shared child care labor more equitably, care would spread laterally instead of being passed down a social-class ladder, diminishing in value along the way. Culturally, Americans have begun to embrace this idea—but they've yet to put it into practice on a truly large scale [see Richard Weissbourd, "Redefining Dad," TAP, December 6, 1999]. This is where norms and policies established in the first world can have perhaps the greatest influence on reducing costs along global care chains.

According to the International Labor Organization, half of the world's women between ages 15 and 64 are working in paid jobs. Between 1960 and 1980, 69 out of 88 countries for which data are available showed a growing proportion of women in paid work (and the rate of increase has skyrocketed since the 1950s in the United States, Scandinavia, and the United Kingdom). If we want developed societies with women doctors, political leaders, teachers, bus drivers, and computer programmers, we will need qualified people to help care for children. And there is no reason why every society cannot enjoy such loving paid child care. It may even remain the case that Vicky Diaz is the best person to provide it. But we would be wise to adopt the perspective of the critical modernist and extend our concern to the potential hidden losers in the care chain. These days, the personal is global.

China's Big Mac Attack[2]

By James L. Watson
Foreign Affairs, May/June 2000

Ronald McDonald Goes To China

Looming over Beijing's choking, bumper-to-bumper traffic, every tenth building seems to sport a giant neon sign advertising American wares: Xerox, Mobil, Kinko's, Northwest Airlines, IBM, Jeep, Gerber, even the Jolly Green Giant. American food chains and beverages are everywhere in central Beijing: Coca-Cola, Starbucks, Kentucky Fried Chicken, Häagen-Dazs, Dunkin' Donuts, Baskin-Robbins, Pepsi, TCBY, Pizza Hut, and of course McDonald's. As of June 1999, McDonald's had opened 235 restaurants in China. Hong Kong alone now boasts 158 McDonald's franchises, one for every 42,000 residents (compared to one for every 30,000 Americans).

Fast food can even trump hard politics. After NATO accidentally bombed the Chinese embassy in Belgrade during the war in Kosovo, Beijing students tried to organize a boycott of American companies in protest. Coca-Cola and McDonald's were at the top of their hit list, but the message seemed not to have reached Beijing's busy consumers: the three McDonald's I visited last July were packed with Chinese tourists, local yuppies, and grandparents treating their "little emperors and empresses" to Happy Meals. The only departure from the familiar American setting was the menu board (which was in Chinese, with English in smaller print) and the jarring sound of Mandarin shouted over cellular phones. People were downing burgers, fries, and Cokes. It was, as Yogi Berra said, déjà vu all over again; I had seen this scene a hundred times before in a dozen countries. Is globalism—and its cultural variant, McDonaldization—the face of the future?

Imperialism And a Side of Fries

American Academe is teeming with theorists who argue that transnational corporations like McDonald's provide the shock troops for a new form of imperialism that is far more successful, and therefore

---

more insidious, than its militarist antecedents. Young people everywhere, the argument goes, are avid consumers of soap operas, music videos, cartoons, electronic games, martial-arts books, celebrity posters, trendy clothing, and faddish hairstyles. To cater to them, shopping malls, supermarkets, amusement parks, and fast-food restaurants are popping up everywhere. Younger consumers are forging transnational bonds of empathy and shared interests that will, it is claimed, transform political alignments in ways that most world leaders—old men who do not read *Wired*—cannot begin to comprehend, let alone control. Government efforts to stop the march of American (and Japanese) pop culture are futile; censorship and trade barriers succeed only in making forbidden films, music, and Web sites irresistible to local youth.

One of the clearest expressions of the "cultural imperialism" hypothesis appeared in a 1996 *New York Times* op-ed by Ronald Steel: "It was never the Soviet Union, but the United States itself that is the true revolutionary power. . . .We purvey a culture based on mass entertainment and mass gratification. . . . The cultural message we transmit through Hollywood and McDonald's goes out across the world to capture, and also to undermine, other societies. . . . Unlike traditional conquerors, we are not content merely to subdue others: We insist that they be like us." In his recent book, *The Lexus and the Olive Tree*, Thomas Friedman presents a more benign view of the global influence of McDonald's. Friedman has long argued in his *New York Times* column that McDonald's and other manifestations of global culture serve the interests of middle classes that are emerging in autocratic, undemocratic societies. Furthermore, he notes, countries that have a McDonald's within their borders have never gone to war against each other. (The NATO war against Serbia would seem to shatter Friedman's Big Mac Law, but he does not give up easily. In his July 2, 1999, column, he argued that the shutdown and rapid reopening of Belgrade's six McDonald's actually prove his point.)

> *If [Ronald] Steel and his ideological allies are correct, McDonald's should be the poster child of cultural imperialism.*

If Steel and his ideological allies are correct, McDonald's should be the poster child of cultural imperialism. McDonald's today has more than 25,000 outlets in 119 countries. Most of the corporation's revenues now come from operations outside the United States, and a new restaurant opens somewhere in the world every 17 hours.

McDonald's makes heroic efforts to ensure that its food looks, feels, and tastes the same everywhere. A Big Mac in Beijing tastes virtually identical to a Big Mac in Boston. Menus vary only when the local market is deemed mature enough to expand beyond burgers and fries. Consumers can enjoy Spicy Wings (red-pepper-laced chicken) in Beijing, kosher Big Macs (minus the cheese) in Jerusalem, vegetable McNuggets in New Delhi, or a McHuevo (a burger with fried egg) in Montevideo. Nonetheless, wherever McDonald's takes root, the core product—at least during the initial phase of operation—is not really the food but the experience of eating in a cheerful, air-conditioned, child-friendly restaurant that offers the revolutionary innovation of clean toilets.

Critics claim that the rapid spread of McDonald's and its fast-food rivals undermines indigenous cuisines and helps create a homogeneous, global culture. Beijing and Hong Kong thus make excellent test cases since they are the dual epicenters of China's haute cuisine (with apologies to Hunan, Sichuan, and Shanghai loyalists). If McDonald's can make inroads in these two markets, it must surely be an unstoppable force that levels cultures. But the truth of this parable of globalization is subtler than that.

The Secret of My Success

How did McDonald's do it? How did a hamburger chain become so prominent in a cultural zone dominated by rice, noodles, fish, and pork? In China, adult consumers often report that they find the taste of fried beef patties strange and unappealing. Why, then, do they come back to McDonald's? And more to the point, why do they encourage their children to eat there?

The history of McDonald's in Hong Kong offers good clues about the mystery of the company's worldwide appeal. When Daniel Ng, an American-trained engineer, opened Hong Kong's first McDonald's in 1975, his local food-industry competitors dismissed the venture as a nonstarter: "Selling hamburgers to Cantonese? You must be joking!" Ng credits his boldness to the fact that he did not have an M.B.A. and had never taken a course in business theory.

During the early years of his franchise, Ng promoted McDonald's as an outpost of American culture, offering authentic hamburgers to "with-it" young people eager to forget that they lived in a tiny colony on the rim of Maoist China. Those who experienced what passed for hamburgers in British Hong Kong during the 1960s and 1970s will appreciate the innovation. Ng made the fateful decision not to compete with Chinese-style fast-food chains that had started a few years earlier (the largest of which, Cafe de Coral, was established in 1969). The signs outside his first restaurants were in English; the Chinese characters for McDonald's (Cantonese Mak-dong-lou, Mandarin Mai-dang-lao) did not appear until the business was safely established. Over a period of 20 years, McDonald's gradually became a mainstay of Hong Kong's middle-class culture. Today the restaurants are packed wall-to-wall with busy commuters, students, and retirees who treat them as homes away from home. A 1997 survey I conducted among Hong Kong university students revealed that few were even aware of the company's American origins. For Hong Kong youth, McDonald's is a familiar institution that offers comfort foods that they have eaten since early childhood.

McDonald's Restaurants by Country (as of June 30, 1999)	
United States	12,490
Japan	2,985
Canada	1,093
Germany	947
Brazil	771
France	744
Taiwan	310
China	235
Italy	211
Hong Kong	158
Other	5,397
Total	25,341

Yunxiang Yan, a UCLA anthropologist, hints that a similar localization process may be underway in Beijing. McDonald's there is still a pricey venue that most Chinese treat as a tourist stop: you haven't really "done" Beijing unless you have visited the Forbidden City, walked around Tiananmen Square, and eaten at the "Golden Arches." Many visitors from the countryside take Big Mac boxes, Coke cups, and napkins home with them as proof that they did it right. Yan also discovered that working-class Beijing residents save up to take their kids to McDonald's and hover over them as they munch. (Later the adults eat in a cheaper, Chinese-style restaurant.) Parents told Yan that they wanted their children to "connect" with the world outside China. To them, McDonald's was an important stop on the way to Harvard Business School or the MIT labs. Yan has since discovered that local yuppies are beginning to eat Big Macs regularly. In 20 years, he predicts, young people in Beijing (like their counterparts in Hong Kong today) will not even care about the foreign origin of McDonald's, which will be serving ordinary food to people more interested in getting a quick meal than in having a cultural experience. The key to this process of localization is China's changing family system and the emergence of a "singleton" (only-child) subculture.

The Little Emperors

In China, as in other parts of East Asia, the startup date for McDonald's corresponds to the emergence of a new class of consumers with money to spend on family entertainment. Rising incomes are dramatically changing lifestyles, especially among younger couples in China's major cities. Decisions about jobs and purchases no longer require consultations with an extended network of parents, grandparents, adult siblings, and other kin. More married women in Hong Kong, Beijing, and Shanghai work outside the home, which in turn affects child-rearing practices, residence patterns, and gender relations. At least in the larger cities, men no longer rule the roost. One of China's most popular television shows features a search for the "ideal husband," a man who does the shopping, washes the

---

In China, as in other parts of East Asia, the startup date for McDonald's corresponds to the emergence of a new class of consumers with money to spend on family entertainment.

---

dishes, and changes the baby's diapers—behavior inconceivable in Mao's heyday.

Most Chinese newlyweds are choosing to create their own homes, thereby separating themselves from parents and in-laws. The traditional system of living with the groom's parents is dying out fast, even in the Chinese countryside. Recent research in Shanghai and Dalian (and Taipei) shows that professional couples prefer to live near the wife's mother, often in the same apartment complex. The crucial consideration is household labor—child care, cooking, shopping, washing, and cleaning. With both husband and wife working full time, someone has to do it, and the wife's mother is considered more reliable (and less trouble) than the husband's mother, who would expect her daughter-in-law to be subservient.

In response to these social and economic changes, a new Chinese family system is emerging that focuses on the needs and aspirations of the married couple—the conjugal unit. Conjugality brings with it a package of attitudes and practices that undermine traditional Chinese views regarding filial piety and Confucianism. Should younger couples strive, irrespective of personal cost, to promote the welfare of the larger kin group and support their aging parents? Or should they concentrate on building a comfortable life for themselves and their offspring? Increasingly, the balance is shifting toward conjugality and away from the Confucian norms that guided earlier generations.

The shift also coincides with a dramatic decline in China's birth rate and a rise in the amount of money and attention lavished on children. The Communist Party's single-child family policy has helped produce a generation of "little emperors and empresses," each commanding the undivided affection and economic support of two parents and (if lucky) four grandparents. The Chinese press is awash with articles bemoaning the rise of singletons who are selfish, maladjusted, and spoiled beyond repair—although psychologists working on China's singletons find them little different from their American or European counterparts.

McDonald's opened in Beijing in 1992, a time when changes in family values were matched by a sustained economic boom. The startup date also coincided with a public "fever" for all things American—sports, clothing, films, food, and so on. American-style birthday parties became key to the company's expansion strategy. Prior to the arrival of McDonald's, festivities marking youngsters' specific birth dates were unknown in most of East Asia. In Hong Kong, for instance, lunar-calendar dates of birth were recorded for use in later life—to help match prospective marriage partners' horoscopes or choose an auspicious burial date. Until the late 1970s and early 1980s, most people paid little attention to their calendar birth date if they remembered it at all. McDonald's and its rivals now promote the birthday party—complete with cake, candles, and silly hats—in television advertising aimed directly at kids.

Prior to the arrival of McDonald's, festivities marking youngsters' specific birth dates were unknown in most of East Asia.

McDonald's also introduced other localized innovations that appeal to younger customers. In Beijing, Ronald McDonald (a.k.a. Uncle McDonald) is paired with an Aunt McDonald whose job is to entertain children and help flustered parents. All over East Asia, McDonald's offers a party package that includes food, cake, gifts, toys, and the exclusive use of a children's enclosure sometimes known as the Ronald Room. Birthday parties are all the rage for upwardly mobile youngsters in Hong Kong, Beijing, and Shanghai. Given that most people in these cities live in tiny, overcrowded flats, the local Kentucky Fried Chicken or McDonald's is a convenient and welcoming place for family celebrations.

For the first time in Chinese history, children matter not simply as future providers but as full-scale consumers who command respect in today's economy. Until the 1980s, kids rarely ate outside the home. When they did, they were expected to eat what was put in front of them. The idea that children might actually order their own food would have shocked most adults; only foreign youngsters were permitted to make their opinions known in public, which scandalized everyone within earshot. Today children have money in their pockets, most of which they spend on snacks. New industries and a specialized service sector have emerged to feed this category of consumers, as the anthropologist Jun Jing has noted in his new book, *Feeding China's Little Emperors*. In effect, the fast-food industry helped start a consumer revolution by encouraging children as young as three or four to march up to the counter, slap down their money, and choose their own food.

In Hong Kong, McDonald's has become so popular that parents use visits to their neighborhood outlet as a reward for good behavior

> *In Hong Kong, McDonald's has become so popular that parents use visits to their neighborhood outlet as a reward for good behavior or academic achievement.*

or academic achievement. An old friend told me that withholding McDonald's visits was the only threat that registered with his wayward son. "It is my nuclear deterrent," he said.

McDonald's could not have succeeded in East Asia without appealing to new generations of consumers—children from 3 to 13 and their harried, stressed-out parents. No amount of stealth advertising or brilliant promotions could have done the trick alone. The fast-food industry did not create a market where none existed; it responded to an opportunity presented by the collapse of an outdated Confucian family system. In effect, McDonald's tailgated the family revolution as it swept through East Asia, first in Japan and Hong Kong (1970s), then in Taiwan and South Korea (1980s), and finally in China (1990s). There is no great mystery here, unless one is predisposed to seeing imperialist plots behind every successful business.

Grimace

In 1994 students protesting against California's Proposition 187, which restricted state services to immigrants, ransacked a McDonald's in Mexico City, scrawling "Yankee go home" on the windows. In August 1999 French farmers dumped tons of manure and rotting apricots in front of their local McDonald's to protest U.S. sanctions on European food imports. During the past five years,

McDonald's restaurants have been the targets of violent protests—including bombings—in over 50 countries, in cities including Rome, Macao, Rio de Janeiro, Prague, London, and Jakarta.

Why McDonald's? Other transnationals—notably Coca-Cola, Disney, and Pepsi—also draw the ire of anti-American demonstrators, but no other company can compete with the "Golden Arches." McDonald's is often the preferred site for anti-American demonstrations even in places where the local embassies are easy to get at. McDonald's is more than a purveyor of food; it is a saturated symbol for everything that environmentalists, protectionists, and anticapitalist activists find objectionable about American culture. McDonald's even stands out in the physical landscape, marked by its distinctive double-arched logo and characteristic design. Like the Stars and Stripes, the Big Mac stands for America.

Despite the symbolic load it carries, McDonald's can hardly be held responsible for the wholesale subversion of local cuisines, as its many critics claim. In China's larger cities, traditional specialties are supported by middle-class connoisseurs who treat eating out as a hobby and a diversion. Beijing's food scene today is a gourmet's paradise compared to the grim days of Maoist egalitarianism, when China's public canteens gave real meaning to the term "industrialized food." Party leaders may have enjoyed haute cuisine on the sly, but for most people, eating extravagantly was a counterrevolutionary crime. During the 1960s, refugee chefs kept microregional specialties alive in the back streets of Hong Kong and Taipei, where Panyu-style seafood, Shandong noodles, and Shunde vegetarian delights could be had at less than a dollar a head. Today, many Cantonese and Taiwanese lament the old refugees' retirement and complain that no one has carried on their culinary traditions; the chefs' own children, of course, have become brokers, lawyers, and professors.

Meanwhile, there has been an explosion of exotic new cuisines in China's cities: Thai, Malaysian, Indonesian, French, Spanish, Nepali, Mexican, and Hong Kong's latest hit, Louisiana creole. Chinese-style restaurants must now compete with these "ethnic" newcomers in a vast smorgasbord. The arrival of fast food is only one dimension of a much larger Chinese trend toward the culinary adventurism associated with rising affluence.

McDonald's has not been entirely passive, as demonstrated by its successful promotion of American-style birthday parties. Some try to tag McDonald's as a polluter and exploiter, but most Chinese consumers see the company as a force for the improvement of urban life. Clean toilets were a welcome development in cities where, until recently, a visit to a public restroom could be harrowing. The chain's preoccupation with cleanliness has raised consumer expectations and forced competitors to provide equally clean facilities. Ray Kroc, the legendary founder of McDonald's, was once asked if he had actually scrubbed out toilets during the early years of his franchise: "You're damn right I did," he shot back, "and I'd clean one today if it needed it." In a 1993 interview, Daniel Ng described his early efforts to import the Kroc ethos to his Hong Kong franchise. After an ineffectual first try, one new employee was ordered to clean the restrooms again. The startled worker replied that the toilets were already cleaner than the collective facilities he used at home. Ng told him that standards at McDonald's were higher and ordered him to do it again.

Another innovation is the line, a social institution that is seldom appreciated until it collapses. When McDonald's opened in Hong Kong, customers clumped around the cash registers, pushing their money over the heads of the people ahead of them—standard procedure in local train stations, banks, and cinemas. McDonald's management appointed an employee (usually a young woman) to act as queue monitor, and within a few months, regular consumers began to enforce the system themselves by glaring at newcomers who had the effrontery to jump ahead. Today the line is an accepted feature of Hong Kong's middle-class culture, and it is making headway in Beijing and Shanghai. Whether or not McDonald's deserves the credit for this particular innovation, many East Asian consumers associate the "Golden Arches" with public civility.

Have It Your Way

At first glance, McDonald's appears to be the quintessential transnational, with its own corporate culture nurtured at Hamburger University in Oak Brook, Illinois. But James Cantalupo, the president of McDonald's Corporation, maintains that his strategy is to become as much a part of local culture as possible and protests when people call McDonald's a multinational or a transnational. "I like to call us multilocal," he told *The Christian Science Monitor* in 1991. McDonald's goes out of its way to find local suppliers whenever it enters a new market. In China, for instance, the company nurtures its own network of russet-potato growers to provide french fries of the requisite length. McDonald's has also learned to rely on self-starters like Daniel Ng to run its foreign franchises—with minimal interference from Oak Brook. Another winning strategy, evident everywhere in East Asia, is promoting promising young "crew" (behind-the-counter) workers into management's ranks. Surprisingly few managers are dispatched from the Illinois headquarters. Yan found only one American, a Chinese-speaker, on McDonald's Beijing management team.

Critics of the fast-food industry assume that corporations always call the shots and that consumers have little choice but to accept what is presented to them. In fact, the process of localization is a two-way street, involving changes in the local culture as well as modifications of the company's standard mode of operation.

The hallmark of the American fast-food business is the displacement of labor costs from the corporation to consumers. For the system to work, consumers must be educated—or "disciplined"—so that they voluntarily fulfill their side of an implicit bargain: we (the corporation) will provide cheap, fast service if you (the customer) carry your own tray, seat yourself, eat quickly, help clean up afterward, and depart promptly to make room for others. Try breaking this contract in Boston or Pittsburgh by spreading out your newspaper and starting to work on a crossword puzzle in McDonald's. You will soon be ousted—politely in Pittsburgh, less so in Boston.

Key elements of McDonald's pan-national system—notably lining up and self-seating—have been readily accepted by consumers throughout East Asia. Other aspects of the Oak Brook model have been rejected, especially those relating to time and space. In Hong Kong, Taipei, and Beijing, consumers have turned their neighborhood restaurants into leisure centers for seniors and after-school clubs for students. Here, "fast" refers to the delivery of food, not its consumption.

Between 3:00 and 5:30 p.m. on Hong Kong weekdays, McDonald's restaurants are invaded by armies of young people in school uniforms. They buy a few fries, pour them out on a tray for communal snacking, and sit for at least an hour—gossiping, studying, and flirting. During the midmorning hours, the restaurants are packed with white-haired retirees who stay even longer, drinking tea or coffee (free refills for senior citizens) and lingering over pancake breakfasts. Many sit alone, reading newspapers provided by the management. Both retirees and students are attracted by the roomy tables, good light, and air-conditioning—a combination not easily found in Hong Kong, Beijing, or Shanghai. In effect, local citizens have appropriated private property and converted it into public space.

The process of localization correlates closely to the maturation of a generation of local people who grew up eating fast food. By the time the children of these pioneer consumers entered the scene, McDonald's was an unremarkable feature of the local landscape. Parents see the restaurants as havens for their school-age children: smoking is banned and (in China and Hong Kong) no alcohol is served, effectively eliminating drugs and gangs. McDonald's has become so local that Hong Kong's youth cannot imagine life without it.

Everyone has heard the story: Japanese little leaguers tour California and spot a McDonald's, whereupon they marvel that America also has Japanese food. Such anecdotes are not apocryphal. The children of visiting colleagues from Taiwan and South Korea were overjoyed when they saw a McDonald's near their temporary homes in the Boston suburbs: "Look! They have our kind of food here," one eight-year-old Korean exclaimed. The stories also work within East Asia: last year, Joe Bosco, an anthropologist at the Chinese University of Hong Kong, took several of his students to Taipei for a study tour. After a week of eating Taiwanese restaurant food, Bosco's charges began to complain that they missed home-style cooking. "Okay," Bosco said, "where do you want to eat tonight?" The students all said, "McDonald's!"

McDonald's has become so local that Hong Kong's youth cannot imagine life without it.

Next to Godliness

In China's increasingly affluent cities, parents now worry more about what their children eat outside the home. Rumors frequently sweep through Beijing and Shanghai with the same story line: migrants from the countryside set up a roadside stall selling youtiar, deep-fried dough sticks eaten with rice gruel for breakfast. To expand the batter, they add industrial detergent to the mix, creating a powerful poison that kills everyone who eats it. Families of the deceased rush back to the scene to discover that the stall has disappeared; the local police are more interested in silencing the survivors than pursuing the culprits. Such stories are, of course, unverifiable, but they carry a "truth" that resists official denials, much like urban legends in the United States. Last summer's food scare in Belgium over dioxin-laced eggs and the recent British mad-cow fiasco were well covered in the Chinese media, feeding the anxieties of urbanites with no reliable system of consumer protection.

McDonald's appeals to China's new elites because its food is safe, clean, and reliable. Western intellectuals may scoff at McDonald's for its unrelenting monotony, but in many parts of the world (including China) this is precisely what consumers find so attractive. Why else would competitors go to such extremes to imitate McDonald's? In Beijing one can find fast-food restaurants with names such as McDucks, Mcdonald's, and Mordornal. In Shanghai a local chain called Nancy's Express used a sign with one leg of the double arches missing, forming an "N." Another popular chain of noodle shops, called Honggaoliang (Red sorghum), advertises itself with a large "H" that bears an uncanny resemblance to the "Golden Arches." All over China, competitors dress their staff in McDonald's-style uniforms and decorate their restaurants in yellow. Corporate mascots inspired by Ronald McDonald—clowns, ducks, cowboys, cats, hamburger figures, mythic heroes, and chickens—parade along the sidewalks of Chinese cities. Local fast-food chains frequently engage in public exhibitions of cleanliness: one worker mops the floors and polishes the windows, all day long, every day. The cleaners usually restrict their efforts to the entryway, where the performance can best be seen by passersby.

So Lonely

During McDonald's first three years in China, Communist Party officials could barely restrain their enthusiasm over this new model of modernization, hygiene, and responsible management. By 1996, however, media enthusiasm cooled as state authorities began to promote an indigenous fast-food industry based on noodles, barbecued meats, soups, and rice pots. Now that McDonald's, Kentucky Fried Chicken, and Pizza Hut had shown the way, party officials reasoned, local chains should take over the mass market. (No such chain has seriously challenged McDonald's, but a Shanghai-based restaurateur has fought a much-reported "battle of the chickens" with KFC.)

Meanwhile, China faces yet another family revolution, this one caused by the graying of the population. In 1998, 10 percent of China's people were over 60; by 2020, the figure is expected to rise to approximately 16 percent. In 2025, there will be 274 million people over 60 in China—more than the entire 1998 U.S. population. Since Beijing has made few provisions for a modern social-security system, the implications are profound. The locus of consumer power will soon shift generations as the parents of today's little emperors retire. Unlike the current generation of retirees—the survivors of Maoism—China's boomers will not be content with 1950s-level pensions, and they cannot expect their children to support them. Like their counterparts in the American Association of Retired Persons, future retirees in China are likely to be a vociferous, aggressive lot who will demand more state resources.

So what will happen to child-centered industries? If its experience in Hong Kong is any guide, McDonald's will survive quite handily as a welcoming retreat from the isolation and loneliness of urban life. The full ramifications of China's single-child policy will not be felt for another 20 years. Having one grandchild for every four grandparents is a recipe for social anomie on a truly massive scale. The consequences of China's demographic time bomb can already be seen on the streets of Hong Kong, where the family began to shrink decades ago. Tens of thousands of retirees roam Hong Kong's air-conditioned shopping malls, congregate in the handful of overcrowded parks, and turn their local McDonald's during the midmorning hours into a substitute for the public gardens, opera theaters, and ancestral halls that sheltered their parents. What stands out at McDonald's is the isolation among Hong Kong elders as they try to entertain themselves. Americans may be bowling alone and worrying about the decline of family life, but in early 21st-century Hong Kong, no one even seems concerned about the emergence of a civil society that ignores the elderly.

Whose Culture Is It, Anyway?

Is McDonald's leading a crusade to create a homogenous, global culture that suits the needs of an advanced capitalist world order? Not really. Today's economic and social realities demand an entirely new approach to global issues that takes consumers' perspectives into account. The explanatory device of "cultural imperialism" is little more than a warmed-over version of the neo-Marxist dependency theories that were popular in the 1960s and 1970s—approaches that do not begin to capture the complexity of today's emerging transnational systems.

The deeper one digs into the personal lives of consumers anywhere, the more complex matters become. People are not the automatons many theorists make them out to be. Hong Kong's discerning consumers have most assuredly not been stripped of their cultural heritage, nor have they become the uncomprehending dupes of transnational corporations.

In places like Hong Kong, it is increasingly difficult to see where the transnational ends and the local begins. Fast food is an excellent case in point: for the children who flock to weekend birthday parties, McDonald's is self-evidently local. Similarly, the Hong Kong elders who use McDonald's as a retreat from the loneliness of urban life could care less about the company's foreign origin. Hong Kong's consumers have made the "Golden Arches" their own.

One might also turn the lens around and take a close look at American society as it enters a new millennium. Chinese food is everywhere, giving McDonald's and KFC a run for their money in such unlikely settings as Moline and Memphis. Mandarin is fast becoming a dominant language in American research laboratories, and Chinese films draw ever more enthusiastic audiences. Last Halloween, every other kid in my Cambridge neighborhood appeared in

(Japanese-inspired) Power Ranger costumes, striking poses that owe more to Bruce Lee than to Batman. Whose culture is it, anyway? If you have to ask, you have already missed the boat.

Customizing the World on the Web[3]

BY ROBIN PEEK
INFORMATION TODAY, MAY 2000

Once upon a time, we were just one great, glorious Web space—borderless, unfettered by rules, a great virtual community. We were so awestruck when creating the Web that we overlooked the fact that this was really a worldwide media platform. Little things—such as requiring visitors to identify themselves as "Mr.," "Mrs.," or "Miss"—may seem innocent, but they may be perceived as insults in certain countries. So we have to get off our little boats circling the "It's a Small World" amusement ride at Disneyland and deal with a truly worldwide and increasingly sophisticated Web.

While it's true that from space the geography is unmarred by borders, in the real world even true Webheads must have passports. Borders are real and meaningful things. Yes, in the U.S. we have been ahead of everyone, but the rest of the world is quickly catching up. For example, *The Standard* (http://www.thestandard.com) recently noted that, due to readily available free Internet access, Net usage in Latin America is projected to explode to 30 million people by 2003.

Real internationalization, not merely having Internet access, is going to make Web life more complicated. And Web-land is already becoming a more formidable place to do business. Search engines don't just find Web sites anymore, as Web-site owners must now agonize to see if they have made the grade (or paid the freight). Click-and-mortar is now reminding the virtual newcomers who really did "get here first." Now Web site owners must determine how (and perhaps even if) they should conduct international activities.

The Border Patrols

We may be seeing the end of the Web's freewheeling ways as more governments take increasingly aggressive postures about the legality (and possible taxation) of the bytes that flow across their borders. That means you could get a friendly (or not so friendly) e-mail

---

message from some government official telling you that you can't say or do or sell something that's on your Web site because it's being viewed in a particular country.

This may come as a surprise to some who believe that because they're moving at "Web speed," the traditional rules somehow don't apply. Perhaps the most widely known example is clothing company Lands' End's recent run-in with the German government, which declared that the company's "lifetime" guarantee on its products is illegal within Germany (14 days is the maximum there). Another example concerns legal mandates, such as the ones in French-speaking Canada that declare that French should not only be available, but also be the dominant language on all publications and signage.

Which brings us to the issue that Web data, like politics, is local. It doesn't matter if your server is located in the U.S.—where your data go, you go. So whether it's paying taxes or conforming to commerce (or publishing) law, if your server is open for business in a particular country, the prevailing wisdom now is to be prepared to have it consider you to be "doing business" within its borders.

Don't Offend the Natives

However, it's not just conforming to local laws but to local customs that should concern contemporary Web publishers. Many traditional publishers are already aware of the necessity of creating separate editions for the global markets. They know all too well that it's not just language but also conventions that must be considered when trying to take a message to a country. Take, for example, numeric conventions, such as currency, measurement, and date/time representations: Does 1/12/00 indicate January 12 or December 1? (Answer: It depends where you are.)

And even though English is the language of the Web, that doesn't mean that readers will stay if an alternative is available. Forrester Research recently reported that people are two times more likely to stay at a Web site if it's written in their native language. While translation programs might be adequate (an 80-to-90-percent accuracy rate is generally reported), most serious Web publishers are reconciling themselves to the fact that content must be completely rewritten in the native language. This customization may even have to conform to an individual country. While both the Portuguese and Brazilians speak Portuguese, there are significant differences in the use of the language.

Unfortunately, there are no translation programs that ensure graphics and visual elements will translate into other cultures, either. In the U.S., for example, orange is considered a warm color, but in Japan it's a cool color. The significance of a shamrock as a good luck charm is lost on most non-Western cultures. An advertising symbol, say the sock puppet currently used by pets.com, has no meaning to those who have not seen the television advertisements.

A Customized Future

The solution is neither easy nor cheap, but it can be found in customization. A customized server can take incoming requests and direct them (using the address of request) to specific sets of pages. So if you are looking for http://www.infotoday.com while in a cyber-cafe in Portugal, your request would serve up pages customized for Portugal. The server that contains the data could be in New Jersey (where the publisher is located), or it could be in Portugal.

It's a competitive world out there and the Web site that best gets the message across wins.

Customization introduces its own set of problems, not the least of which is that it utterly destroys any notion of one universal Web. And a user could be barred from getting to particular pages (even if a person knew that the pages existed). In theory, a company could refuse to serve up any pages to a particular country if legal or taxation reasons demanded it.

A big issue that's facing Web publishers will be the control of content. If all content is housed within one server or server farm, the content can be easily controlled by that entity. One downside of this model is the logic of keeping the data closer to the requester, so if someone in Argentina requests a page, the transactions don't have to travel to the U.S. This proximity, of course, speeds up delivery—which is the name of the virtual game in Web-land. But, not surprisingly, surrendering server control makes people nervous, particularly with Internet laws being as ill-defined as they are right now.

Letting content be controlled locally can help ensure that viewers get a cogent message (which is the whole point of publishing). But it has the potential of raising havoc with establishing or maintaining a clear corporate image or message. In addition, data may not be consistently maintained. Information may be released in the U.S. on Monday, but not translated for one country until Tuesday and another on Thursday. On the other hand, it's a competitive world out there and the Web site that best gets the message across wins.

Despite all the problems it will introduce, it seems inevitable that we are facing a customized future. It appears unlikely that the world is just going to start singing in harmony and come to agreement on contentious issues (like privacy and data security). And yes, I shudder when I think about how bogged down the Web is going to become as legal beagles start combing through Web sites trying to ensure that everything complies.

But, it is indeed called the World Wide Web, and it seems inevitable that eventually the world is going to catch up and bring real-world issues along. It is, as the song goes, "a small world after all."

We Can Fight, We Can Win[4]

Effective Protest Efforts Range from Comic Books to Boycotts

BY SARAH ANDERSON AND JOHN CAVANAGH WITH THEA LEE
THE NATION, DECEMBER 6, 1999

There is nothing inevitable about the current direction of globalization. Yes, corporations have used their tremendous power to shape many of the rules of the road for globalization to meet their own narrow interests. In the nineties they have escalated their efforts with sweeping new rules at the local, national and global levels to enhance their mobility across borders.

And yet in the United States and elsewhere, this decade has also been one of growing resistance to global corporations. Even among the elite stalwarts of trade and investment liberalization, the long-standing free-market consensus appears to be unraveling. Except for the rigid IMF and U.S. Treasury Department, two sets of pro-globalization academic and political leaders have broken away. One remains committed to liberalization of trade flows but, in light of the global financial crisis, calls for controls on short-term capital flows. The other calls for abolition of the IMF, arguing that it condones reckless lending by bailing out investors.

The challenge for the future will be to push alternative agendas through this crack in the consensus. Central to these efforts is the belief that trade and investment should not be ends in themselves but tools for promoting ideals such as equality, democracy, good jobs, a clean environment and healthy communities. The goal is to shift from an emphasis on exports based on the plunder of resources and the exploitation of workers to sustainable economic activity that roots capital locally and nationally.

Now is the time for the citizens' backlash to become the "frontlash" for a new global economy. Unions, environmental groups and other citizens' organizations are demanding a place at the negotiating table to craft new rules to guide globalization. And they are taking direct action to make their feelings known.

---

4. Article by Sarah Anderson and John Cavanagh with Thea Lee from *The Nation*, December 6, 1999. Copyright © *The Nation*. Reprinted with permission.

Worker Power

In the late nineties, a reinvigorated U.S. labor movement has increased its efforts in international solidarity work. A prime example is the successful resolution of the 1997 Teamsters strike against the United Parcel Service, in reaction to UPS's plans to shift from full-time to lower-paying, part-time and temporary jobs. While UPS dominates the U.S. market for small-package delivery, the firm is more vulnerable in Europe, where it faces stiff competition. UPS workers in England, Belgium, Germany, the Nether-

---

Citizens in several countries have expressed their resistance to corporate-driven globalization in the voting booth.

---

lands and France supported the U.S. workers by carrying out sympathy strikes, leafleting and other actions. According to then-Teamster international representative Andy Banks, "Enlightened self-interest was the key. European UPS workers and their unions reasoned that if the 185,000 striking Teamsters could not stop the part-time, subcontracting mentality of the company, what could a few hundred or a few thousand workers hope to achieve in the smaller UPS European operations?" During the strike, unions also worked to block UPS deliveries in India, the Philippines and Spain.

Shareholder Power

Members of the Interfaith Center on Corporate Responsibility, an association of nearly 275 religious denominations, submitted 194 shareholder resolutions in one recent year to press for corporate accountability in the areas of the environment, treatment of workers and other subjects. For example, in 1995 the Benedictine Sisters of Boerne, Texas, filed a shareholder resolution with Alcoa requesting that the company pay its Mexican workers adequate wages. With support from ICCR and the Coalition for Justice in the Maquiladoras, two Alcoa workers confronted CEO Paul O'Neill at the company's annual meeting. At first defensive, O'Neill later took steps to improve conditions and increase wages by 20 percent.

Voter Power

Citizens in several countries have expressed their resistance to corporate-driven globalization in the voting booth. For example, in Mexico in 1997, opposition parties critical of the ruling party's economic policies gained control of the lower house of Congress, and opposition leader Cuauhtémoc Cárdenas was elected mayor of Mexico City. As the head of Mexico's largest opposition party during the NAFTA debate, Cárdenas was a strong advocate for an alternative approach to globalization, stressing that trade "must be an instrument of development, not an end in itself."

Consumer Power

One consumer strategy has been to reward corporations employing "good" business practices by allowing such firms to identify their products with a label. The Rugmark campaign, for example, awards a special label to firms that insure that their employees are adults paid at least the local minimum wage. Manufacturers that join Rugmark consent to surprise visits by Rugmark inspectors and local human rights and child advocacy groups. Rugmark also works with U.S. and European importers to provide funding for the education of former child workers in the rug industry. In the United States the campaign is coordinated by the Rugmark Foundation, housed at the International Labor Rights Fund.

Student Power

On more than seventy-five campuses, students have been negotiating with their schools to ban the purchase of products bearing the school logo from factories that violate labor rights. At a number of these universities, students have built support for such a ban by staging fashion shows featuring clothes made in sweatshops. As the models parade down the runway, an announcer describes the conditions under which the clothes were made. The first school to adopt such a code was Duke University, which now forbids suppliers from using child labor and requires them to maintain a safe workplace, pay at least minimum wage, recognize the right to form a union and allow independent plant monitoring. Duke students are continuing to press for an expansion of the code to require suppliers to pay a living wage.

CORPORATE V. COUNTRY ECONOMIC CLOUT—THE TOP 25

Country or Corporation	GDP/sales ($mil)
United States	7,745,705
Japan	4,201,636
Germany	2,100,110
France	1,396,540
United Kingdom	1,271,710
Italy	1,145,370
China	825,020
Brazil	786,466
Canada	603,085
Spain	531,419
South Korea	442,543
Russian Federation	440,562
Australia	391,045
Netherlands	360,472
India	359,812
Mexico	334,766
Argentina	322,730
Switzerland	293,400
Belgium	264,400
Sweden	227,751
Indonesia	214,593
Austria	206,239
Turkey	181,464
General Motors	178,174
Hong Kong	171,401

Sales figures from *Fortune,* April 27, 1998, and *Forbes,* July 27, 1998. GDP figures from World Bank, World Development Report 1998/99, pp. 212-213.

People Power

In 1994, the fiftieth anniversary of the World Bank and IMF, citizens' groups from all over the world organized a "Fifty Years Is Enough" Campaign. In the United States, it has involved more than 200 environmental, development, faith-based, labor and policy organizations. Congress responded to their demands by restricting funding for the agencies until they improved disclosure, environment and resettlement policies, and by requiring that the United States use its voting power in the World Bank to promote internationally recognized workers' rights.

Another mass movement is Jubilee 2000, a coalition of religious and secular groups that has demanded cancellation of much of the debt owed by the poorest countries. Jubilee draws its inspiration from the biblical book of Leviticus, which describes a Year of Jubilee every fifty years in which social inequalities are rectified, slaves are freed, land is returned to original owners and debts are canceled. Jubilee 2000 coalitions exist in dozens of countries.

Artist Power

In Mexico, a superhero named "Superbarrio" fights against injustice on behalf of the poor. Wearing red tights, gold wrestling trunks and a flowing gold cape, Superbarrio is a frequent star of political demonstrations. Under NAFTA, Superbarrio's heroics have taken him on many crusades across the border. Once he swept into Los Angeles to take water samples for toxic testing in Mexican labs (the local environmental group did not trust the results they were getting from the U.S. government). Cartoonists have lent their artistic skills to support educational efforts. A booklet by the Coalition for Justice in the Maquiladoras illustrates common workplace scenarios to help Mexican workers learn about their labor rights so they can more effectively defend themselves against abuses by the primarily U.S.-owned corporations operating on the border.

Political theater has also proved an effective way of educating and mobilizing people around globalization issues. For example, Nepali villagers gather around boomboxes in tea shops to listen to an audiocassette of a play about hydroelectric power, featuring one of Nepal's most famous comedians.

The Protectionist Myth[5]

BY BRUCE STOKES
FOREIGN POLICY, WINTER 1999/2000

Conventional wisdom is always conventional. And it is frequently wrong. Such is the case with the widespread belief among many economists, headline writers, business leaders, and policy makers that free trade is in retreat, imperiling the hard-won gains of past market liberalization, and threatening ruinous trade wars. When the U.S. House of Representatives voted to impose quotas on foreign steel producers in March, *The Economist* mourned that "Americans are beguiled by protectionism." A month later, U.S. Federal Reserve Board Chairman Alan Greenspan echoed that sentiment when he ominously noted, "I am concerned about the recent evident weakening of support for free trade in this country."

News stories from around the world add to these worries: Korean students march in the streets of Seoul urging consumers to buy only Korean products. French farmers trash a McDonald's to retaliate against American trade sanctions and to protest the globalization of their dining experience. Brazilian shoemakers, under threat of sanctions, agree to voluntary quotas on exports to Argentina. Washington and Brussels battle over trade in bananas, hormone-treated beef, and genetically modified organisms (GMOs). The U.S. Congress refuses to grant the American president fast-track trade-negotiating authority. Activists in Great Britain and India destroy fields of bioengineered crops and press for bans on the importation of GMOs. And massive protests by thousands of demonstrators greet trade ministers when they gather in Seattle, Washington, to launch the next round of multilateral trade negotiations.

These anecdotes make arresting headlines and compelling sound bites but paint an inaccurate picture. Free trade is not in retreat. On the contrary, tariffs are declining and trade is expanding almost everywhere. Many types of protectionism—such as export restraints and nontariff barriers—are disappearing. Antidumping actions are on the rise, but the total number of such cases worldwide is still less than in previous years. On the whole, trade has never been freer. And the globalization of capital and technology

5. Article by Bruce Stokes from *Foreign Policy*, Winter 1999/2000. Copyright © Carnegie Endowment for the International Peace. Reprinted with permission.

markets and the creation of the World Trade Organization (WTO) mean that the built-in restraints on imposing new trade barriers have never been greater.

Of course, protectionism could still rear its head. New "voluntary" understandings to limit trade are emerging. The seeds that could flower into future protectionism lie in America's mounting trade imbalance; the rising balance-of-payments problems in Africa, Asia, and Latin America; the mounting toll of unemployment in Japan; and the lack of competitiveness of European agriculture.

As true defenders of orthodoxy, free traders feel compelled to react forcefully to the first signs of apostasy. But such zeal can blind judgment. Crying wolf about false chimeras of protectionism impugns credibility. It also reflects a zealot's insensitivity to the plight of individual workers and communities whose lives have been changed

---

The insistence that the new battles are really just an extension of the old war reflects free traders' denial of the growing complexity of the global economy they have created.

---

forever by international competition. And it suggests an ideological disdain for the give-and-take of real life, where political compromises and strategic backsliding are needed to achieve progress.

By needlessly sounding the protectionist alarm, advocates of freer trade risk dulling the sensitivity of policy makers and the public to less understood but ultimately more serious threats to the future of international commerce. Rising concern about the fate of the free market often confuses manifestations of "new" protectionism (efforts to use trade sanctions to enforce labor, environmental, and health standards) with "old" protectionism (efforts to protect the narrow economic interests of one industry at the expense of another). The insistence that the new battles are really just an extension of the old war reflects free traders' denial of the growing complexity of the global economy they have created. Such arrogance and insensitivity risk allowing new problems to fester and eventually to pose the very threats to open markets that defenders of the free-trade faith aver they are trying to avoid.

What Protectionist Upsurge?

The continual expansion of world trade should speak for itself. Even with the contraction of many Asian economies and a slowdown in world economic growth, the volume of trade in goods and services still grew by 3.6 percent in 1998. It is expected to grow by 3.7 percent in 1999 and jump by 6.2 percent in 2000. The culprit for the slowdown was anemic growth in key economies—such as Japan, where a second year of recession led to a 5.5 percent contraction in imports. Protectionism was not a major impediment to imports in its traditional lairs: Imports grew in 1998 by 10.5 percent in Canada and the United States and by 7.5 percent in the European Union, both rates of growth well above their average increase during the 1990s. Despite global economic troubles, Latin America, long a bastion of protectionism, saw imports grow by 9.5 percent in 1998, and the countries of the former Soviet bloc increased imports by 10 percent.

The implacable march of global commerce is due, in part, to the widening engagement of many developing countries in the trading system. And this growing economic integration reflects the fact that traditional protectionism—manifested in high tariffs and non-tariff trade barriers such as voluntary export restraints, countervailing duties, and antidumping measures—has not increased significantly around the world in recent years.

Thanks to commitments made in the Uruguay Round of multilateral trade negotiations, tariffs have been cut across the board and now cannot legally be raised on items accounting for 87 percent of all merchandise trade, up from 73 percent a decade ago. It is true that, in the wake of the Asian crisis, Ecuador, Malaysia, Mexico, the Philippines, Thailand, and Venezuela all raised some tariffs. For the most part, these were increases of duties from their actual to their bound tariff rates, in effect applying the higher duty that individual governments agreed to in the Uruguay Round, rather than the lower rate that many have been applying in recent years. Such a move is a reversal in recent trends, but it is in keeping with international commitments. And such increases often have had greater symbolic than statistical significance. For example, average tariffs in Latin America are still about half of what they were in the early 1980s.

Voluntary export restraints (VERS)—agreements by exporting countries to circumscribe shipment of a particular product to another country, usually to head off the imposition of an even more onerous import quota or other trade restraint—were the protectionist weapon of choice in the 1980s. By 1992, Europe had 33 such restrictive agreements and the United States had 17, including a ceiling on imports of Japanese cars. Today, these protectionist measures have almost disappeared. Only one significant European VER remains, and it will be eliminated by the end of this year thanks to commitments made in the Uruguay Round.

More broadly, other nontariff trade barriers, including import licensing and discriminatory import fees—both designed to discourage imports—are being phased out. The share of tariff lines that have at least 1 nontariff barrier associated with them has diminished in Europe from about 1 out of 10 to less than 1 out of 30, and in the United States from about 1 out of 10 to 1 out of 20. In the mid-1980s, nontariff barriers existed for nearly all tariff lines in Central American countries and for 60 percent of tariff lines in South American nations. Today such impediments to trade affect less than 10 percent of tariff lines in the region.

Similarly, in 1990, more than three quarters of all African countries had trade regimes classified as "restrictive" by the International Monetary Fund. By the beginning of 1999, the proportion of "restrictive" regimes had fallen to 28 percent. The number of antidumping cases initiated by Australia fell from 213 in the period 1991-94 to 77 in the period 1995-98. During the same two periods, Canada cut the number of its cases from 84 to 39 and Mexico from 127 to 31. Brazil initiated 23 countervailing duty investigations between 1992 and 1994, but none from 1995 to 1997. Nowhere is this decade-long shift more evident than in the United States, which is most frequently the target of protectionist finger-pointing. In the 1980s, Washington had restraints on imports of autos, steel, machine tools, and motorcycles, among other things. Most such restraints are now gone.

In 1998, the United States initiated 36 antidumping investigations, more than double the number in 1997. An additional 44 were begun in the first seven months of 1999. These filings—particularly on various types of steel imports—have been exhibit number one for free traders arguing that protectionism is on the increase. But equally notable are the antidumping cases that were not filed. At the time of the steel cases, trade lawyers in Washington darkly forecast formal charges concerning the dumping of machine tools, semiconductors, and other goods. The cases never materialized. More broadly, the total number of U.S. antidumping cases in 1998 was less than half the number of investigations launched in either 1992 or 1986. And even at 1999's accelerated pace, the total for the year is likely to fall short of previous highs. Finally, any assessment of antidumping trends in the United States must measure the net, not the gross, number of cases. In 1998, 25 antidumping duty orders were revoked, more than the total revocations in the three prior years combined.

Passage of the steel-quota legislation by the U.S. House of Representatives is also frequently cited as evidence of America turning its back on free trade. Clearly the bill had protectionist intent and, most likely, violated U.S. international commitments. But it was also a free vote. Legislators could curry favor with constituents by voting for the bill, knowing full well that President Clinton had said he would veto it. In the end, the Senate never allowed a vote on the legislation, calling into question widespread lamentations about Congress' inherently protectionist nature.

Similarly, congressional failure to grant fast-track trade-negotiating authority has been widely cited as a sign of declining support for free trade on Capitol Hill. But the blame for the failure to pass fast track in recent years lies not with reluctant members of Congress, but mostly with the White House and the American business community, who have failed to push for it sufficiently. Few Washington observers believe Congress will deny the president trade-negotiating authority once there are tangible benefits to be obtained in concrete negotiations.

Globalization Mitigates Protectionism

The rapid globalization of domestic economies over the past decade—and the resulting increase in competition from imports—has obviously fueled protectionist demands in many countries. However, both the highly integrated nature of the modern world economy and the recent profusion of international commitments governing trade serve to mitigate the kind of virulent protectionism that has been seen in the past.

Of course, it would be folly to assume that protectionism is now impossible just because it is irrational. Such logic has never prevailed. But it is also shortsighted not to acknowledge just how much more difficult and costly protectionism is today than it was two generations ago. Trade represents a growing share of the world economy. Merchandise trade accounted for 37 percent of global gross domestic product (GDP) in 1998, up from 27 percent in 1980. Any future interruption of that commerce would have a greater impact on economic growth than ever before.

More important, changes in the nature of the world's largest market have created previously nonexistent American domestic political support for trade. In 1993, for example, imports accounted for a quarter of U.S. consumption of autos, auto parts, and machinery. And imports are generally credited with having helped keep U.S. inflation in check and with providing the competition that has recently spurred American productivity. As a result, the import lobby in Washington has become formidable. Users of imported steel are recognized as having forced an end to U.S. restraints on foreign imports, and auto dealers selling imported cars were a major voice in the fight to avoid duties on imported Japanese luxury cars in 1995.

Other nations have made hard-to-reverse commitments to open markets. Since 1994, when Mexico entered the North American Free Trade Agreement with Canada and the United States, it has signed free-trade deals with Bolivia, Chile, Colombia, Costa Rica, Nicaragua, and Venezuela. Its trade has mushroomed as a result, and exports, which in 1993 accounted for 15 percent of GDP, now make up 30 percent of the economy. With trade and related foreign investment generating about a million jobs, more and more businesses and workers have a vested interest in opposing trade impediments.

The changing composition of trade has also taken some of the steam out of protectionist pressures. The rising share of manufactured products as a portion of trade (manufactured goods accounted for a little over half of U.S. trade in 1909 and over four fifths today)

With trade and related foreign investment generating about a million jobs, more and more businesses and workers have a vested interest in opposing trade impediments.

---

explains public resistance in Europe, Japan, and the United States to imports of steel, textiles, and other traditional manufactured products. But more and more of this trade consists of intra-industry exchanges, meaning it involves component parts necessary for more advanced products (in 1995, 78 percent of U.S. trade was intra-industry compared with 53 percent in 1909). As a result, despite public opposition to manufactured imports, the nature of this trade makes it increasingly difficult to single out foreigners for blame or to devise protectionist policies that do not simply end up hurting a country's own companies.

The modern reality of who trades with whom also serves to check protectionism. Three fifths of U.S. imports come from Canada, Europe, and Japan, denting the protectionist argument that trade enables low-wage countries to undermine production in industrial economies. Moreover, four fifths of U.S. exports are bought by other advanced nations, making any American flirtation with protectionism particularly vulnerable to crippling retaliation. European nations are even more dependent on each other for trade, making it virtually impossible to translate the European public's nationalist proclivities into protectionist policies.

Protectionism is also simply harder to impose in today's global economy because international trade rules are much more stringent than they were just a decade ago. Commitments made in the Uruguay Round make it difficult to erect traditional trade barriers: Export restraints are being phased out, and other procedures have been tightened. The EU has agreed to cut its average tariffs on manufactured goods from 5.7 percent to 3.6 percent. Canada will slash average duties on manufactured goods from 9 percent to 4.8 percent. Finally, the existence of the WTO dispute settlement mechanism exerts new discipline on national trade practices. The WTO has mandated an end to Europe's discriminatory banana import regime. In response to EU complaints against the United States, it is reviewing the legality of the infamous Section 301 of the 1974 Trade Act. In the 1980s, alleging "unfair" foreign trade practices, Washington used the 301 provision repeatedly to impose or threaten to impose duties on shipments from other countries.

The Seeds of Future Protectionism

It would, of course, be Pollyannaish to assume that protectionism is dead [see Table]. The demonstrable waning of American protectionist fervor in recent years is in part a function of the prolonged strength of the American economy. Growth will eventually slow, joblessness will rise, and the U.S. trade deficit, which will approach a record $300 billion in 1999 if current trends continue, will likely again become a source of public concern. In that environment, latent reservations about free trade will be exploited by protectionist politicians, such as Reform Party presidential aspirant Patrick Buchanan. In Japan, recent record high unemployment and continued dismal economic prospects are only likely to reinforce governmental and public support for the relatively closed nature of the domestic market. Europe's refusal to accelerate the pace for dismantling its Common Agricultural Policy—especially its export subsidies—will continue to stiffen opposition to further trade liberalization among American farmers and others.

In Latin America, market opening in the past decade is increasingly blamed for rising current account deficits and growing disparties in income. Free trade's price tag and the failure to share the benefits of economic reform have already stirred political turmoil in Venezuela and could fuel a renaissance of inward-looking tendencies elsewhere in the region. Argentina's threat to impose limits on imports of Brazilian products in the wake of that country's devaluation was a warning of the kind of protectionist backlash that economic turbulence could trigger. The demand by developing countries that their exports and markets be accorded "special and differential" treatment in the upcoming multilateral trade negotiations threatens to relegitimize protectionist practices done away with in the Uruguay Round.

China's emergence as a major player in the global marketplace poses additional challenges. The county's substantial export capability threatens widespread displacement of other developing country producers in industrial nation markets, and China's rapidly rising trade surplus with the United States could eventually become a rallying cry for protectionist interests.

More broadly, the new information economy (along with the emergence of electronic commerce) is a fertile field for subtle and innovative forms of protectionism. European rules on the transborder transfer of data, created to safeguard privacy, inhibit the competitive advantage of American service companies. Regulations in parts of Asia that curtail direct delivery of products purchased on the World Wide Web may keep European and American companies from circumventing dysfunctional distribution systems that have long served as effective protectionist barriers. And taxes on Internet transactions and failure to protect intellectual property on the Web could nip electronic commerce in the bud.

> *The new information economy (along with the emergence of electronic commerce) is a fertile field for subtle and innovative forms of protectionism.*

Thus, although the conventional wisdom about a protectionist upsurge is clearly wrong, the seeds of future protectionism do exist and bear close watching. In addition, there are other, new issues emerging onto the trade agenda that may pose even greater long-term threats. The way in which the champions of free trade respond to these new threats may ultimately prove most important for the future of international commerce.

Confronting the "New Protectionism"

The new protectionism has its roots in mounting consumer fears of genetically modified organisms, environmentalists' desire to preserve biodiversity, and union concerns about child labor and poor working conditions. Whatever their provenance, all trade barriers have a protectionist effect. Safeguarding domestic farmers from foreign competitors who have access to bioengineered seeds or banning importation of rugs made by children distorts the market by favoring one set of producers over another.

This new protectionism—with its reliance on import bans and quotas—can often look very much like the old variety. But it is both analytically and politically unsound to confuse the two. The very emergence of consumer, labor, and environmental concerns reflects the successful deepening of global economic integration. Trade now touches more and more lives in more and more ways. As a result, new issues such as intellectual property and trade in services unavoidably emerge. Their insertion into the trade policy mix has complicated matters for trade negotiators and created new opportunities for protectionist actions. But these are signs of the success of globalization, not its failure. Similarly, that industrial country environmentalists now worry whether shrimp traps in developing countries inadvertently kill sea turtles is not a sign of rising protectionism. It reflects the emergence, in an increasingly transparent world, of a global market for shrimp caught by developing countries.

New economic opportunities create new economic vulnerabilities, and if advocates of free trade want the benefits of a market economy, then they must be willing to accept the complications that come with it. They ignore this new complexity, and the give-and-take necessary to deal with it effectively, at their peril. Whether environmental, labor, or consumer concerns become full-blown protectionism depends on whether free traders are willing to meaningfully engage these concerns. If child labor and GMOs are simply dismissed as thinly veiled efforts to safeguard domestic producers, public frustration with globalization will only grow.

In sounding the alarm about a looming protectionist menace, free traders pose a real danger to free and open markets, because raising such a false alarm only inhibits trade negotiators and elected leaders from risking further trade liberalizations. Already averse to such risk, these skittish officials will then lack the ambition and vision needed to ensure that the upcoming round of multilateral trade negotiations continues the extraordinarily successful postwar expansion of global commerce. The cost of these foregone future benefits of market liberalization could far exceed any current economic threats from renewed protectionism.

The onus of avoiding a protectionist resurgence rests squarely with those who want more open markets. The coming round of global trade negotiations provides an opportunity to dispel developing country dissatisfaction with the liberal trading order by finally dismantling industrial country trade barriers that impede imports of African, Asian, and Latin American agricultural products, light industrial goods, and textiles and apparel. The round can provide the setting for a global dialogue on the problems posed by the rapid emergence of electronic commerce—privacy, preservation of indigenous culture, and the transitional challenges facing traditional retailers. In recognition that further market liberalization may not be politically feasible without first addressing the plight of those disadvantaged by globalization, the negotiations can embrace,

Down in the Dumps		
Type of Economy	**Number of Antidumping Initiations**	
	1991-94	**1995-98**
Developed Economies		
Australia	213	77
Canada	84	39
European Union	135	122
United States	226	94
All developed economies	678	353
Developing Economies		
Argentina	59	72
Brazil	59	54
India	15	78
Korea	14	34
Mexico	127	31
South Africa	16	72
All developing economies	394	509

Source: WTO Secretariat, Rules Division; Antidumping Measures Databases.

rather than dismiss, the legitimate concerns of consumers, environmentalists, and labor unions. By further lowering tariffs, ending export subsidies, and extending the reach of trade rules in the service sector, negotiators can stimulate global commerce, increasing the beneficiaries of trade and undermining support for protectionism. And by strengthening and making the WTO dispute settlement procedures more transparent, the new round can restore public faith that the global marketplace will function fairly.

Protectionism is not yet on the rise. The alleged evidence of its revival and the demonstrations in Seattle are merely warning signs. The benefits of international commerce are not yet adequately shared, the costs are not yet sufficiently compensated, and the full impact of trade on the environment has not yet been taken into account. If these problems are not dealt with, protectionism could return with a vengeance in the first years of the new millennium, with devastating consequences. But the world would not have wild-eyed economic nationalists to blame. The villains would be short-sighted free traders who choose to fret about nonexistent protectionism today, rather than work to head off the true threat tomorrow.

III. Who's in Charge? Governing a Global Society

Editor's Introduction

Expanded trade between countries and a decrease in the number of protective measures instituted by individual nations has brought an increase in international interaction. Trade disputes and altercations have arisen, matched by the proliferation of large-scale international crime organizations. This increased interaction between countries has necessitated an agreement on a global governing body to set conditions, mediate quarrels, and enforce standards. At the end of World War II, the allied forces established an international court system to punish perpetrators of war crimes and crimes against humanity. They also decided that war-torn Europe would need some help regaining its footing, so they created two institutions—the International Monetary Fund (IMF) and the World Bank—to lend money to nations in need. In 1947 they signed a General Agreement on Trade and Tariffs (more commonly referred to as GATT), which finally solidified, in 1995, into the World Trade Organization, or WTO. Numerous other global organizations exist as well. NATO, the European Union (EU), and Interpol, for example, have conducted business in some form or another for some time now.

Not everyone has been happy with these solutions. Criticisms of global governance range from the general to the more specific (detractors of the WTO, for example, often descry that organization's policy of ignoring environmental and human rights concerns in order to focus exclusively on issues of free trade). In particular, many people are concerned that global governing bodies will eventually usurp the sovereignty of individual nations. They fear that bureaucrats, who do not need to endure an election process to sit on these governing institutions, will decide with whom each country can do business and on what terms. R. C. Longworth, in his article "A New Kind of War" (from the *Bulletin of the Atomic Scientists*), explores this conflict between the need for governance and fear of losing individual sovereignty. Using the recent war in Kosovo as a focal point, he sets up a dichotomy between Serbia, fighting to preserve a nation state, and NATO, an alliance of countries that have agreed to pool their sovereign rights (such as controlling their own militaries) in order to work toward a common goal. He suggests that the nation state will never die out altogether, but there will be a shift toward a loose global governing structure.

Robert Wright agrees with Longworth's assessment. In the article "Continental Drift," which appears in the *New Republic*, he writes that though pundits may label anti-globalization protestors as hyper-anxious flakes, the protesters are right to declare that the WTO is, in fact and in deed, a global governing body. He agrees that governance on a global scale will eventually coalesce, but it will not, he writes, overtake the sovereignty of nation states. His essay includes reviews of many of the global bodies, such as the WTO, IMF, and EU.

The third article in this section shifts the focus away from tensions between nation states and global bodies and concentrates, instead, on the details of the global institutions. In "There's Something Happening Here" (published in *Fortune*), Jerry Useem describes the history, interactions, and work methods of several such governing bodies, including the IMF, World Bank, and the WTO, and concludes that officials should listen to criticisms by protesters if they wish to improve the global institutions.

Wolfgang H. Reinicke's essay, "The Other World Wide Web: Global Public Policy Networks" (from *Foreign Policy*), looks at constructive ways ordinary citizens can change the directions of global governing institutions. Observing that change is really a bottom-up process (rather than imposed from the top down), he finds that networks that bring together nongovernmental organizations (NGOs), national governments, and researchers, among other groups, can cut through bureaucratic red tape and help advise policy makers, who can't possibly have time to specialize in all the issues pertaining to and stemming from globalization.

In addition to hammering out new laws by which to interact politically on a global scale, a similar need has arisen for new organizations to address the age-old problem of crime. John Lloyd ("The Godfathers Go Global," *New Statesman*) explains that organized crime has become a global operation, and it has done so much more quickly and efficiently than crime fighting organizations. To combat this new enemy, national policing organizations (such as the FBI) have formed cooperative agreements with their foreign counterparts. Lloyd describes the cooperation of formerly separate, national crime fighting institutions and identifies five organized crime "fever spots."

The last article in this section, "The Man from Interpol," published in *CIO Magazine*, reviews the current state of affairs at the world's premier crime fighting organization. Contrary to popular rumor, Interpol is not a syndicate of high-technology spies but a network of national police forces. Alice Dragoon interviews Peter Nevitt, the director of Interpol's Information Systems department. Nevitt explains Interpol's history of crime fighting, the methods for sharing information between its member countries, and the place that technology holds in fighting drug trafficking, fraud, and art heists.

A New Kind of War[1]

BY R. C. LONGWORTH
BULLETIN OF THE ATOMIC SCIENTISTS, JULY/AUGUST 1999

From NATO's point of view, Slobodan Milosevic's attempt to drive ethnic Albanians from Kosovo was a dangerous anachronism in a globalizing world.

Right on cue, just as the millennial midnight was about to strike, NATO entered a new legal and strategic world. The battle for Kosovo was both the result of global pressures that have been building for a decade now, and a precedent for a future that is only dimly perceived.

Like most explorers in a new world, the NATO nations are making this one up as they go along.

The issue is sovereignty—what does it mean and who has it? Is it absolute? If not, when can it be violated, and by whom? Who decides?

Czech President Vaclav Havel, talking about the NATO bombing of Serbia in a speech to the Canadian parliament, said that "blind love for one's own country . . . has necessarily become a dangerous anachronism, a source of conflict, and, in extreme cases, of immense human suffering." We live, Havel said, in a new world "in which all of us must begin to bear responsibility for everything that occurs."

"In such a world," he said, "the idol of state sovereignty must inevitably dissolve. With this transformation, the idea of noninterference—the notion that it is none of our business what happens in another country and whether human rights are violated in that country—should also vanish down the trapdoor of history."

State sovereignty, enshrined at the Peace of Westphalia more than 350 years ago, became absolute in this century. We recognized foreign governments when they controlled their own territories, and we granted them the right to do anything within their own borders as long as they did not infringe the borders of their neighbors. Violations of frontiers were a cause of war; violations within frontiers were not.

Given the holocausts, pogroms, cultural revolutions, and gulags of the twentieth century, this doctrine of absolute sovereignty left a lot to be desired. But it was what we had, the basis of the interna-

---

1. Article by R. C. Longworth from the *Bulletin of the Atomic Scientists*, July/August 1999. Copyright © *Bulletin of the Atomic Scientist*. Reprinted with permission.

tional system and a useful tool. The Soviet Union rejected any Western criticism of its regime as "an impermissible interference in the internal affairs of a sovereign country." Mostly, we went along with this, because the alternative could upset a nuclear balance that trumped all other issues, including human rights.

The Effects of Globalization

That era ended 10 years ago, and in the past decade the concept of sovereignty has changed, but the change has never been dramatized as starkly as last spring. The Balkan war was truly the last twentieth-century war.

On one side was Serbia, fighting for territory, frontiers, and sovereignty in a globalizing world where such concepts just weren't that important any more. The Serb cause was powered by the memories of 600-year-old defeats, of blood grievances against neighbors, of a conviction that ancestral lands were too important to be shared with tribes speaking a different language or professing a different religion.

In a globalizing world, brains and communications are important, land is not.

On the other side was NATO, a multinational alliance of 19 nations that had agreed to share, to a greater or lesser degree, their defenses, which is one of the key attributes of national sovereignty. NATO said it fought for human rights, or to excise an infection from the European body, or to protect its own credibility, or out of simple revulsion at the sight of Europeans being jammed into railway cars 55 years after that sort of thing was supposed to have ended forever.

What it was not fighting for was land, or conquest, or oil, or empire. That last empire, the Soviet one, is dead, and no one is building another. In a globalizing world, brains and communications are important, land is not.

The globalization of the world, in fact, is the key to what's going on in the Balkans. The war, in a way, was an atavism in a world of global markets and global cooperation, with money and jobs and ideas flying across frontiers as though they didn't exist. Of the 19 NATO nations, 11 are consciously submerging their sovereignty—even their currencies—into a new, borderless economic and political bloc, the European Union.

Even more important is the fact that all the Balkan countries except Serbia long to join the EU. This is astonishing, given the extreme nationalism for which the Balkans are notorious. But all the other Balkan nations—Macedonia, Albania, Bulgaria, Romania, Croatia, Slovenia, probably Montenegro if and when it breaks free of Serbia—have either applied for EU membership or say they will.

This desire is having amazing and positive consequences. For the first time in their history, many Balkan nations are behaving in a most UN-Balkan way. Romania has agreed to stop persecuting its Hungarian minority. Macedonia and Greece have agreed to disagree on their dispute over Greece's challenge to Macedonia's name. Bulgaria and Macedonia have settled their argument over whether the Macedonian language is a separate language or is only a Bulgarian dialect. An Albanian political party is part of the governing coalition in Macedonia, as is a Turkish party in Bulgaria.

To much of the world, these concessions to sweet reason may seem marginal. In the Balkans, they are seminal. The Bulgarian-Macedonian language dispute, for instance, held up the signing of treaties between the two neighbors, because they could not agree which languages should be used. The solution: an agreement earlier this year to write the treaties in the languages of the two countries, which amounts to a Bulgarian recognition of Macedonian as a separate tongue. It's not that Bulgarians really believe that Macedonian is separate from Bulgarian. They don't. But they have agreed that the dispute—which has enormous psychological meaning for people in this area—will not stand in the way of progress.

The Balkan Carrot

Bulgaria, Macedonia, and the other Balkan nations are willing to take these steps—to put their Balkan past behind them, in effect—because they so desperately crave NATO and EU membership and know the only way to get it is to convince Brussels that they are modern nations. It is the same lure that persuaded other ex-communist nations like Poland, Hungary, and the Czech Republic to break with their own pasts and adopt both democracy and market economies. The reward for the Poles, Hungarians, and Czechs has been acceptance into the Western family of nations. Now the Balkans want in, too, and they know what they have to do. NATO membership could be near for many of these Balkan nations although, given the state of their economies, EU membership is probably a generation away. But the promise of membership and progress toward that goal will be a powerful incentive.

Sali Berisha, the former president of Albania, said "the EU is a model for us. It asks us to give up some of our sovereignty, but it works. It means integration and cooperation."

"The Balkans today are not about borders but about what kinds of states are going to flourish in the region and about the chances of the region to be part of the new Europe," said Ivan Krustev, director of the Center for Liberal Studies in Bulgaria.

But the war was precisely about borders. Was Kosovo part of Serbia or not? Could Serbs and ethnic Albanians live within the same borders? Would Kosovo be independent, with its own borders, or only autonomous, within Serbian borders? Would new borders be drawn, partitioning it?

"It is precisely the fears of exclusion from Europe that command the behavior of governments and publics," Krustev concluded.

The Unpunishable Crime

Slobodan Milosevic has committed many crimes. But he will nut be tried in The Hague for one of the worst, the hurling of his explosive nationalism into this attempt by the other Balkan countries to turn themselves into mature European nations. Serbia stands, both geographically and politically, astride the routes connecting the Balkans to Brussels. No Balkan economy could thrive as long as Milosevic prosecuted his wars, scattered hundreds of thousands of refugees into countries that could barely support their own people, and continued to fertilize the ethnic rivalries that fueled the conflict.

The fear and hate spread by Milosevic has deeply affected a new generation of Kosovar Albanians, who are ready to retaliate and fight. "I never remember when I could go out and feel secure," said 19-year-old Memli Krasniqi, a Kosovar refugee now in Tetovo, Macedonia. Locked in the idleness of exile during the war, he and his friends spent their days in a pizzeria on the main street of this western Macedonian city, drinking strong coffee, smoking, and talking about revenge.

"We tried to live a normal life," said Krasniqi, "but it was a fake life. If I saw a policeman, I'd cross over so I wouldn't meet him. He'd stop me, beat me, take my money. This is not just the last year, it's the last 10 years."

A State of Mind

If and when Milosevic goes, the Serbian people themselves must come to terms with their own past and decide if they, too, want to be a normal European nation. Currently, Serbia has a foot in both worlds, the old one driven by nationalism and ethnic rivalries, and the modern European one of which so many Balkan people want to be part.

The Balkans, as a state of mind and geography, embrace Greece, the European portion of Turkey, Bulgaria, Romania, Albania, and the shards of Yugoslavia—not only Serbia and Montenegro, but the new ex-Yugoslav nations of Macedonia, Croatia, Slovenia, and the various pieces of Bosnia-Herzegovina.

The region's history mixes long periods of oppression—500 years under the Ottomans, 50 years under the Soviets—with spasms of tribal wars, terrorism, refugee flows, shifting borders, mighty empires, misery, foreign intervention, all stored up in conflicting memories to be used as the excuse for the next battle.

Can we blame all of Serbia's present problems, however, on Milosevic? The Serbian people were given a choice 10 years ago between the Balkan past and a European future. Three times, by

---

Currently, Serbia has a foot in both worlds, the old one driven by nationalism and ethnic rivalries, and the modern European one of which so many Balkan people want to be part.

---

voting for a Milosevic government, they chose the past. Nothing good will happen in the Balkans until the Serbs accept the enormity of their nation's crimes and, like the Germans after World War II, opt for the new world, born from the end of the Cold War and the rise of the global economy.

Crumbling Sovereignty

Much has been said about how the global economy saps national sovereignty by taking control of currencies and economies from national governments and giving it to global markets and traders. The financial crises in Asia, Brazil, and Russia portrayed this loss of economic sovereignty.

Less discussed is the way that political sovereignty—the right and ability of governments to run their own countries their own way, without outside interference—also is crumbling.

By the time the Soviet Union collapsed and died, the global economy was already nibbling at economic sovereignty. Erosion of political sovereignty swiftly followed.

The United Nations, led by Russia and the United States, began authorizing interventions in other countries to settle civil wars or cure ethnic outrages. Sometimes, as in El Salvador or Cambodia, the countries agreed. Sometimes, as in Somalia, there was no government to agree.

In 1991, after the Gulf War, the victorious powers, using U.N. authority, set aside no-fly zones in Iraq where planes belonging to that nation's government could not fly. This was the international community ignoring national sovereignty for humanitarian reasons: in this case, the persecution of the Kurds by Saddam Hussein.

Other interventions followed, in places like Rwanda and Bosnia. International monitors began passing judgment on whether Third World elections met democratic standards. A former dictator, Gen. Augusto Pinochet, was jailed in Britain on the basis of charges filed in Spain for acts committed in his own country, Chile; British courts have ruled he must be extradited to Spain. An international court, the very one that has now indicted Milosevic and his aides, was set up in The Hague to judge accused Yugoslav war criminals.

> *"The suffering of [oppressed minorities] is so much more important than sovereignty."*— **Kofi Annan, U.N. secretary general.**

The U.N. Contradiction

Clearly, the old idea of absolute sovereignty was giving way to a new world where concern for human rights limited sovereignty and made it conditional on the good opinion of the world community. Kofi Annan, now the U.N. secretary general, told me in 1993 that "sovereignty cannot be absolute. . . . There are very few issues that one can really say are internal. . . . The suffering of [oppressed minorities] is so much more important than sovereignty."

These earlier incursions into sovereignty took place under U.N. authority. But the U.N. itself is based on "the sovereign equality of all peace-loving states." Its charter says that members "shall refrain . . . from the threat or use of force against the territorial integrity or political independence of any state."

But the charter also pledges members "to take joint and separate actions" to uphold "universal respect for, and observance of, human rights and fundamental freedoms for all."

So what if the only way to protect human rights and freedoms is to use force against the territory of another nation?

That was the Kosovo rub. In this turn-of-the-millennium era, when human rights may trump sovereignty, it may only be possible to uphold the U.N. Charter by breaking it.

This is what happened in Iraq, with Security Council approval. But Russia and China threatened to veto any repeat of that precedent, especially in Kosovo. It was the Western community—represented by NATO—not the international community, that decided that Serbia had forfeited the right to sovereignty by its actions within its own borders against some of its own citizens, the Kosovar Albanians. Thus has the right of intervention devolved down from the world community to the Western alliance.

In the past, nations went to war to defend their "vital national interests." In this case, NATO went to war not because of the national interests of any of its 19 members but to defend the civilization of the West.

Philip Stephens, writing in the *Financial Times* of London, said that "this war has marked out with awkward clarity the irresistible tension between two distinct forms of international law. The first, and most familiar, of these is that of the United Nations Charter designed to preserve the territorial integrity of sovereign states. The second, born at Nuremberg and developed subsequently in international conventions against genocide and torture, hold that there are some crimes which transcend the inviolability of national states."

The Nuremberg standard, established by the Nazi war crimes trials in 1946, lay dormant through the Cold War. Now it rules international affairs.

Humanitarian Precedents

This is a new world. The Greek newspaper, *Kathimerini*, wrote that "today's policy is a legitimizing precedent for the future." In the future, if some NATO allies like Greece refuse to go along with a U.S.-led humanitarian intervention, would the United States and a few allies have the right to act? Or the United States alone? And, if so, would this right also belong to, say, China?

Greece belongs to NATO, but *Kathimerini*, like most Greeks, disapproved of this NATO intervention because it has its own border problems—a dispute with Turkey over ownership of 200 Aegean islands—and worried that any NATO-sponsored border changes in Kosovo would give Turkey an excuse to move in. But its fears of a precedent were legitimate. In truth, no one yet understands this new world and where it is going.

In Kosovo, Serbia and Greece speak for the twentieth century, which has been the heyday of the nation-state. NATO speaks for the twenty-first century, which will be global, for better or for worse, and will pay less attention to borders, sovereignty, and who owns the Aegean islands.

Havel, in his speech in Canada, also saw an "important precedent for the future" in the NATO intervention. But, unlike *Kathimerini,* he found the philosophical and humanitarian justification overwhelming:

"It has been clearly said that it is simply not permissible to murder people, to drive them from their homes, to torture them, and to confiscate their property. What has been demonstrated here is the fact that human rights are indivisible and that, if injustice is done to one, it is done to all."

Continental Drift[2]

World Government Is Coming. Deal with It.

BY ROBERT WRIGHT
NEW REPUBLIC, JANUARY 17, 2000

In recent years, more and more people have raised the specter of world government. Ralph Nader, protesters in Seattle, Pat Buchanan, militiamen in the heartland—all sense an alarming concentration of planetary power in one or more acronyms: WTO, U.N., IMF, and so forth.

Of course, these people have something else in common: They are widely considered fringe characters—flaky, if not loony. And their eccentric visions have been punctured by legions of sober observers. "The WTO is not a world government," an economist wrote in a *Wall Street Journal* op-ed last month after the Seattle protests against the World Trade Organization. His verdict has been echoed by various academics and pundits.

But this may be one of those cases when the flaky are closer to the truth than the sober. Much power now vested in the nation-state is indeed starting to migrate to international institutions, and one of these is the WTO. This doesn't mean that two or three decades from now we'll see world government in the classic sense of the term—a single, central planetary authority. But world government of a meaningful if more diffuse sort is probably in the cards. It follows from basic technological trends and stubborn economic and political logic. And, what's more, it's a good idea. Among other virtues, it could keep a sizable chunk of the liberal coalition from veering off toward Buchananism.

If the political forces driving the WTO toward firmer and broader authority seem less than overwhelming, one reason is that the key political players have a love-hate relationship with world government and tend to dwell on the hate part.

Many on the left, when denouncing the WTO, talk as if national sovereignty were sacred. The WTO, Nader has long complained, "means foreign regulation of America. It means any two dictatorships can out-vote us. . . . It means secret tribunals can rule against our laws." Yet Nader and most of the Seattle left would

---

gladly accept a sovereignty-crushing world body if it followed the leftish model of supranational governance found in the European Union. Indeed, it was partly to please the Seattle activists that President Clinton espoused a future WTO whose member nations would meet global environmental and labor standards or else face sanction.

Many centrist and conservative free-traders also talk as if national sovereignty should be inviolable. They were aghast at Clinton's proposal to take the WTO "beyond its proper competence," as an editorial in *The Economist* sternly put it. But they can live with sovereignty infringement of a less leftish variety—the kind that erodes a nation's power to erect subtle trade barriers via environmental or health policy. They certainly didn't lose sleep over the famous 1998 case in which the United States, under threat of WTO sanction, relaxed its ban on shrimp caught in nets that kill sea turtles.

Of course, these free-traders deny that this sort of ruling amounts to world government. *The Economist* editorial said that "the WTO is not a global government" but merely a place where nations "make agreements, and then subject themselves to arbitration in the event of a dispute." But isn't that a large part of what a government is: a body whose constituents agree to respect its authority, to accept punishment if they're deemed to have broken the rules?

Assorted other players, such as human rights hawks, also have mixed feelings about world government. After Seattle, William Safire wrote a column backing Clinton's view that the WTO should someday punish nations that exploit child labor. This is quite a turnaround: Safire, a longtime free-trader and something of a libertarian, now believes that foreigners in Geneva should decide whether you can buy a soccer ball made in Pakistan. Struggling to contain his cognitive dissonance, Safire issued a disclaimer: "I am not a global warmnik. . . . Indeed, laissez-fairies have always been dancing in my garden." If I were Safire, I'd peek out at my garden to see whether the fairies are still in a festive mood.

For all these people—traditional leftists, centrist and right-wing free-traders, and assorted single-issue agitators (everyone except the Buchananites, basically)—the fundamental question has been settled. They agree that sometimes nations should surrender an appreciable chunk of sovereignty to a central authority. They just disagree on when. Even as they heap scorn on the notion of world government, they're really arguing about what kind of world government we should have.

The evolution of world government has two basic engines—stubborn economic logic and stubborn political logic, both fueled by technology's relentless shrinking of the economic distance between nations.

The economic logic is pretty simple. You could describe it as a series of non-zero-sum games—a series of cases in which nations, to achieve win-win outcomes or avoid lose-lose outcomes, enmesh themselves in common governance. The series starts with that elementally human non-zero-sum game, mutually profitable exchange. Nations trade with one another. Then they see further gains in agreements that will mutually lower tariffs (game number two). Then they decide all would benefit by dampening quarrels over what constitutes a violation of the rules, so they set up a way to handle disputes (game number three). Crossing this last threshold—forming an inchoate judiciary—is what turned the General Agreement on Tariffs and Trade into the World Trade Organization.

But adjudication entails tricky questions. For example: How do you handle covert trade barriers? When a country makes it illegal to import shrimp caught in nets that kill sea turtles, is that just an environmental law? Or is it de facto protectionism, as the WTO claimed when it demanded that the United States quit barring shrimp imports from several Asian nations? In theory, the United States could have ignored the ruling. All the WTO would have done in response would have been to approve retaliatory tariffs by aggrieved countries. Still, the United States has benefited from so many WTO rulings that it has a stake in preserving respect for them. That's the way good government works: A central authority, by solving non-zero-sum problems, gives out in benefits more than it exacts in costs, thus justifying its existence. This net benefit is why WTO rulings will probably become more binding, whether through sheer custom or through tougher sanctions.

The WTO isn't breaking new ground here. It's following in the footsteps of a body that's much further down the road of supranational governance: the European Union. Europe is the most geographically dense conglomeration of high-tech nations in the world. So, as technology shrinks economic distance, Europe is on the leading edge of the trend. That doesn't mean that its political present is the world's political future. The EU has been shaped by various elements peculiar to European history (including a dogged post-1945 desire to avoid war). Still, it may offer a hint of things to come.

For example: With transnational commerce growing, all of Europe's national currencies became a bother. There was costly currency conversion and uncertainty about exchange rates. So the

EU opted for a single currency. And one currency meant one central bank; each nation lost its autonomous central bank and, at a more symbolic level, its currency (or, as they aptly say in Britain, its sovereign). At this point—with nations surrendering control over their monetary policy—the line between a loose association of nations and an outright confederacy has arguably been crossed.

As Europe was unifying its currencies, *The Economist* published an article called "One World, One Money," noting the analogously powerful logic behind global monetary union. The article stressed the political difficulty of such a goal, and some economists doubt its economic wisdom as well. Still, as exchange rates gyrated after the Asian financial crisis, there was talk in both Argentina and Mexico about adopting the U.S. dollar as official currency.

The EU also gets involved in regulatory issues, from food labeling to health and labor law. (It decided that member states could—and,

---

The question is whether at the global level ... politics will dictate the construction of a substantial body of law.

---

indeed, must!—permit the sale of Viagra.) Right-wing free-traders claim there is no sound economic rationale for this sort of meddling. They say that the EU's attempt to specify everything from cheese labels to the maximum length of the workweek represents the triumph of interest-group politics. In some cases, at least, this is true; a maximum workweek doesn't follow from Econ 101 principles about maximizing GDP. But so what? Interest-group politics has always been part of governance. At the local and national levels, much of government consists of services rendered to various groups in order to maintain their support for the larger governmental enterprise. The question is whether at the global level, too, politics will dictate the construction of a substantial body of law.

There is reason to think so, and much of it was on display in Seattle. Well-organized interest groups in affluent nations fear—correctly, in many cases—that they'll be hurt by the continued lowering of trade barriers. So they want to thwart further lowering unless they get global rules that will blunt its impact, such as the rules Clinton has now embraced.

Can these groups really hold trade liberalization hostage to their agenda? Absolutely. In 1997, Clinton introduced fast-track legislation, which denies Congress the power to amend negotiated trade deals before voting on them—and which, practically speaking, is a prerequisite for passing most trade accords. Bowing to Republican pressure, Clinton phrased the legislation narrowly: it wouldn't have allowed U.S. negotiators to include labor and environmental rules in trade agreements. Liberal interest groups responded by defeating the bill. So for now, at least, America's real-world political choice seems to be either trade liberalization that invites lefty supranational governance or no trade liberalization. Both Democratic presidential candidates seem to favor the former option, and, if elected, each of them would presumably seek the leftish fast-track authority that Clinton didn't seek.

In the short run, this authority would yield little. Developing nations generally oppose global environmental and labor law, which raises production costs and thus dulls their factories' competitive edge. Still, there are two reasons this obstacle will probably prove temporary. First, the United States and other rich nations, with markets that poorer nations lust after, have tremendous bargaining power. Second, as time passes, the developing

---

In coming years, expect workers in poor nations to link up with Western labor groups to pursue their common cause: higher wages in poor nations.

---

nations will themselves develop strong constituencies for left-leaning world law.

This second point was lost in the post-Seattle commentary. Negotiators for developing nations went on television and alleged that American union leaders, with their poignant pleas for better working conditions abroad, were phonies; they were at heart worried not about protecting foreign workers but about making foreign labor more pricey and hence less competitive internationally.

Absolutely true. In fact, many American workers would love to price foreign workers out of the market entirely. But they never will. A more realistic goal is to *slightly* raise labor costs abroad. And, if they do that, they'll have most foreign workers on their side. Sure, a few children will lose their jobs if child labor is regulated. And, sure, if workers in poor nations are guaranteed the right to organize, the result could be a minimum wage that would put a few adult workers out of jobs. But the American minimum wage has the same effect, and most workers still support it, for quite rational reasons.

So, in coming years, expect workers in poor nations to link up with Western labor groups to pursue their common cause: higher wages in poor nations. The groups won't see eye-to-eye on everything. American workers would like to raise environmental standards abroad as a way to increase production costs, whereas foreign workers will prefer the sort of raised production costs that mean higher wages. Still, there will be enough common interest that, to some extent, workers of the world will unite—if not exactly in the context Marx envisioned.

Other international coalitions will also blossom. Western environmentalists, for example, share an interest with Third World tourist industries in cleaning up Third World cities.

As international lobby groups acquire power and start doing the things national lobby groups have long done, economists and industrialists will grumble about the costs. The special interests, they'll say, are gumming up the works, dulling capitalism's edge, slowing down globalization!

And it will be true. But is that so bad? Globalization has polluted developing nations, dislocated workers in developed nations, and radicalized some environmentalists and religious fundamentalists. And radicalism is a special problem when, thanks to advancing weapons technology, any two or three highly alienated people can create a pretty lethal terrorist cell.

What is really happening is that political globalization is catching up to economic globalization.

Don't get me wrong. Globalization is great. On balance, it makes the world's poor people less poor (a fact that doesn't seem to have penetrated the brain of the average Seattle protester). And it fosters a fine-grained economic interdependence that makes war among nations less thinkable. But these benefits are all the more reason to keep globalization from getting derailed by the reactionary backlash it incites when it moves too fast. And derailment is possible. As Paul Krugman recently noted in *The New York Times,* the "First Global Economy"—the one that took shape in the late nineteenth century—foundered early this century in part because its constituency didn't extend very far beyond a cosmopolitan elite.

Nor is the derailment of globalization per se the only thing to worry about. Some historians trace the virulence of twentieth-century German nationalism to the nineteenth century, when industrialization swept from west to east, leaving bewilderment in its wake. And Russia, even more than Germany, had to fast-forward from an age of serfs into the industrial revolution—and, in a sense, it never recovered, never got fitting governance. It got Stalin instead.

In a way, it's a misnomer to speak of slowing globalization. After all, the things that might do the slowing—supranational labor or environmental groups, global bodies of governance—are themselves part of globalization. What is really happening is that *political* globalization is catching up to economic globalization.

This has a precedent on a smaller scale. In the United States during the early twentieth century, as economic activity migrated from the state to the national level, the national government grew powerful enough to regulate it. Some of these regulations made simple economic sense, but some of them—labor laws in particular—were political in rationale and had the effect of subduing capitalism, dulling its harsher edges. This was, among other things, a preemptive strike against Marxist revolution—against the turmoil that unbridled modernization can bring—and a successful one. Enlightened capitalists realized that giving labor a seat at the table would help make the world safe for capitalism.

By the same token, enlightened capitalists should today invite the Seattle protesters indoors. One way or another, people who feel threatened by globalization will make their influence felt. Either they'll modulate globalization by linking up with like-minded groups abroad to help shape international rules or they'll take the economic-nationalist route and lobby for the sort of trade barriers that, in addition to starting trade wars, often involve xenophobia and nativism. The way to keep these people from being sheer protectionists—and, in some cases, from morphing into full-fledged Buchananites—is to turn them into WTO lobbyists, which means making the WTO a body worth lobbying. Put suits on those scraggly rabble-rousers and send them to Geneva!

The WTO, though the topic of world governance du jour, is hardly the only global institution with real economic power. The International Monetary Fund (IMF) makes loans to troubled nations to prevent panics—the rough analogue of a nation's bank-deposit insurance—and in return asks for sound management and transparent bookkeeping. This may not sound very forceful. But to lend when the private sector refuses to do so is to subsidize, and with subsidy comes power. Much of the U.S. government's power over states, after all, consists not of legalized coercion but of strings attached to subsidies.

After the Asian crisis, some economists argued that the IMF had been too heavy-handed—that it shouldn't demand fiscal austerity so single-mindedly and that by too readily bailing out bad investors it encouraged more bad investment. But almost no one is saying the IMF should quit lending altogether, and almost no one is saying it should quit using its lending as leverage of one sort or another. As with the WTO, the mainstream argument isn't about whether to have a form of world government but about what form of it to have.

And, as with the WTO, the reason to expect the IMF's ongoing solidification is simple. Its authority results from shrinking economic distance. This shrinkage is the reason economic downturns can be contagious, the reason rich nations suddenly care about the financial soundness of poor nations. And if there is one thing the basic direction of technological change clearly implies, it is continued shrinkage—more interdependence among nations.

For that matter, the shrinkage of noneconomic distance will also continue. A decade from now, global laws regulating the prescription of antibiotics could make sense, if the too-casual use of these drugs creates strains of super-bacteria that can cross oceans on airplanes. And then there is cyberspace, that notorious distance-shrinker and sovereignty sapper. It empowers offshore tax-evaders, offshore libelers, offshore copyright-violators. Nations will find it harder and harder to enforce more and more laws unless they coordinate law enforcement and, in some cases, the laws themselves.

But, even given all these reasons for firmer and broader global governance, will it ever get as firm and broad as the governance of nation-states? Probably not. World government may well always

---

We do face what you could call planetary security problems, and they will help sustain the current drift toward real, if loose, world government.

---

rely on member states to levy its sanctions. It will probably never inspire the patriotic fervor nations do. And it may always be diffuse, consisting of lots of partly overlapping bodies: some regional, some global; some economic, some environmental; some comprising national governments, some comprising nongovernmental organizations.

Why won't world government ever be as taut as old-fashioned national government? For one thing, governments have traditionally drawn internal strength from external opposition. If you scan the historical and prehistoric record for distant parallels to the current moment, the nearest approximations you'll find are when agrarian villages have united to form "chiefdoms" or when chiefdoms evolved into ancient states. And there are no clear examples of such transitions happening in the absence of external hostility. For a full-fledged global political conglomeration to take place without the threat of war against a common foe would mark a contrast with all of the known past. And, barring an invasion from outer space, no such threat will be available.

Still, we do face what you could call planetary security problems, and they will help sustain the current drift toward real, if loose, world government. Impending climate change may not have quite the viscerally galvanizing effect of troops massed on your border, but it does qualify as a common peril best combated by concerted action. Terrorism is also a common peril (and, actually, a pretty galvanizing one). As more compact, lethal, and long-range weapons make terrorists tougher, national governance will become less and less adequate to the task of national security.

Already, with the Chemical Weapons Convention, the United States has agreed to international inspections intrusive enough to have filled the Senate chamber with plaints about surrendered sovereignty. But the surrender (a minor one, in truth) was rational; permitting such inspections on our soil is the only way to get them to happen on foreign soil. And chemical weapons are just the beginning. Biological weapons are orders of magnitude more lethal and much easier to make covertly. The encroachment on sovereignty that combating them will require is, to current sensibilities, shocking. But the idea of trauma—say, 20,000 deaths in an American city—has a way of making the unthinkable widely thought.

As technology pulls and pushes nations together, it highlights an irony: world government, which for so long was a pet cause of the idealistic left—the "woolly minded one-worlders"—isn't getting much support from the left. True, some Seattle activists profess a willingness to work with a left-leaning WTO. But when Naderite Lori Wallach declared, "We're the coalition that's going to tell the WTO, 'You're going to be fixed or you're going to be nixed,'" her heart seemed to be with the "nixed" part. Certainly that was the sentiment of the average Seattle protester.

But, even if nixing were within the left's power, it would be a mistake. Stopping the WTO in its tracks wouldn't turn back the clock. Under current tariff levels, globalization would continue (and, besides, tariffs would probably keep dropping via bilateral trade deals). The various problems that exercise the left—environmental decline, an exodus of low-skill jobs from high-wage nations, human rights violations—would persist.

And these problems are just about impossible to solve without an enforcement mechanism—without the power of sanction that the WTO, more than any other world body, has to offer. The Rio accords on global warming, for example, lack an enforcement mechanism and are notable for the blithe disregard with which various signatories have treated them. The history of international labor accords tells the same story. After the Seattle talks, a *New York Times* editorial said that "the administration can urge other groups, like the International Labor Organization, to pursue the issue with or without the WTO's participation." Which is to say, with or without effect. The ILO has been in existence for 81 years and, lacking the force of sanction, has been unable to do much of anything.

One oddity in contemporary political nomenclature is the tendency of leftist economic nationalists, who favor raising tariffs, to call themselves "progressives." Early this century, progressives were people who realized that communications and transportation technologies were pushing the compass of economic activity outward, from individual states to the United States. In response, they pushed economic regulation from the state to the federal level. The modern-day successors to these progressives should be advocating supranational regulation, not impeding it with unilateral tariffs.

Seattle may have moved them in that direction. At the end of the week, however virulent the anti-WTO rhetoric remained, the "progressive" left was thinking more seriously about using the WTO as a vehicle for its agenda. One big reason was Bill Clinton. For an American president to say that global laws on the treatment of workers should be enforced with real sanctions authorized by a worldwide body was a milestone in the evolution of global governance.

Clinton's remarks have been dismissed as a transparent ploy to lock up the labor vote for Al Gore, as a nostalgic effort to bond with 1960s-esque protesters, and as a tactical blunder that alienated negotiators from poor nations. All of this may be true. But it's also true that these days Clinton is said to be preoccupied with his legacy, trying to pave the way for a thumbs-up verdict from historians a generation hence. If so, then one-worlders should be cheered by his Seattle performance. No one has ever accused Bill Clinton of not knowing which way the wind is blowing.

There's Something Happening Here[3]

BY JERRY USEEM
FORTUNE, MAY 15, 2000

Around 1 P.M. on Monday, April 17, a woman with a foam ever-green tree on her head stood before a police barricade on Washington's Pennsylvania Avenue, picked up a bullhorn, and asked several hundred protesters to repeat after her. "We the people"—"We the people"—"are going to enter"—"are going to enter"—"the World Bank"—"the World Bank"—"and IMF meetings"—"and IMF meetings." The police, looking weird and foreboding with their riot gear, gas masks, and armored vehicle, politely demurred. "That isn't going to happen," said one.

A line of protesters advanced anyway, arms locked and chanting, "Nonviolence!" A few confusing moments later nightsticks were swinging and the protesters were falling back amid a cloud of pepper spray. A bullhorn nearby began blaring the Darth Vader theme from *Star Wars.*

That was just one moment of many during the rain-soaked festival of protest against the World Bank and International Monetary Fund—a festival of ragtag activists who arrived with a variety of beefs (hormone-free, of course) and got arrested and occasionally beaten for their trouble. But less remarked upon—and far more troubling, in the end—was the beating the protesters suffered at the hands of mainstream pundits.

Some of this was to be expected; as targets go, the protesters were about as fat as they come. Their economics were often mixed up. They attracted a fringe of anarchists and down-with-capitalism types. They used the word "evil" a lot. And, let's face it, a grown man dressed up as a sea turtle just looks funny.

Still, the intellectual pig pile that ensued was startling in its ferocity. Global Village Idiots, snarled the *Wall Street Journal,* which mocked the protesters for "bringing their bibs and bottles to the nation's capital this week." *Newsweek* contemptuously dismissed the event as a "parody of protest" staged by shiftless Dead-heads "who have virtually no grasp of the issues."

---

3. Article by Jerry Useem from *Fortune,* May 15, 2000. Copyright © *Fortune.* Reprinted with permission.

The *New York Times* op-ed page, too, was a broth of invective, launching no fewer than three broadsides. David Frum, in a vacuous bit of redbaiting, argued that because socialism had failed, "people like the Washington protesters are left with nothing constructive to say about poverty and development." The influential foreign affairs columnist Thomas Friedman, last heard trashing Seattle's WTO protesters as "a Noah's ark of flat-earth advocates, protectionist trade unions, and yuppies looking for their 1960's fix," wasn't much kinder.

What these globalization troubadours seem to find especially galling are alarmist statements like "The current situation condemns hundreds of millions of people to unnecessary suffering and millions to premature death, and [the World Bank and IMF] are parties to the disaster." Or moralistic declarations like "It is high time that we take the IMF seriously—seriously enough to hold it accountable for its actions, its failed forecasts, and the details of the 'advice' that it imposes on the developing world."

But those aren't the words of some window-smashing crank. They're quotes from Jeffrey Sachs, the Harvard economist—the first from a speech he delivered to the World Bank a couple of days after the April protest, the second from a 1998 article he wrote for *The American Prospect.*

Lest we forget, Sachs is no foaming radical; he was closely associated with the "shock therapy" reforms administered to the former Soviet bloc. But he's willing to concede what the know-it-all commentators, in their rush to educate the masses, won't: The protesters have a point. A good point. A point that cuts to crucial questions about what the global economy will look like, how it will be governed, and whose interests it will serve. Their new breed of economic activism has appeared not only in Seattle but also in Davos, Switzerland; the City, London; and now Washington, D.C. It represents nothing less than a challenge to the "Washington Consensus" —the shorthand favored by global technocrats to describe the triumphalist mix of free markets and American-led turbocapitalism that has fueled policymaking for the past decade.

In short, the movement appears to have legs. The world's financial and corporate elites would do well to listen up.

But first, to address the question everyone is asking: Who are these people? To hear most pundits tell it, the average protester was a wild-eyed protectionist/Luddite in thrall to both Pat Buchanan and the vegan lobby. Paul Krugman, the MIT economist and *Times* op-ed contributor, even coined a name for this pathetic woodland creature: Seattle Man.

This makes for a wonderful straw adversary, but Seattle Man bears little resemblance to any of the people I met in the streets over four days. Most were young, most were moralistic, many were attached to "affinity groups" with goofball names like the Groucho Monarchs. Yet very few were peddling economic autarky as the solution to the world's problems.

Nevertheless, beneath the cavalcade of cliches—the Che Guevara flags, the "Times They Are a-Changin'" sing-alongs—there was a heady sense of their having found the common denominator, perhaps even a Grand Unified Theory of protest. "A lot of people think this might be the thing of our generation," gushed Russell Cote, a student at Seton Hall Law School.

That thing, of course, is "globalization," loosely defined as the system of worldwide integration by which goods, capital, and labor are free to move across national borders. Most of the protesters said they didn't object to this system per se; they seemed to have been sufficiently drilled in their economics classes on free trade's very substantial benefits. But they objected to the system's more deleterious effects, such as the widening income gaps among and within countries, which many studies have traced to globalization. (However, it's also true that most of those studies also link globalization to higher overall growth rates.) More controversially, the rabble said they stood for the right of "indigenous peoples" to balance the priorities of their local, if somewhat inefficient, economies against the relatively theoretical dictates of a hyperrational global marketplace. Their motto could well have been a flip-flop of the usual call to arms: THINK LOCALLY. ACT GLOBALLY.

> *"A lot of people think this [globalization] might be the thing of our generation."*—
> **Russell Cote, Seton Hall Law School student.**

The institutions at issue in D.C.—primarily the World Bank and IMF—struck many observers as odd targets. After all, a sign beside the entrance to the Bank reads, OUR DREAM IS A WORLD WITHOUT POVERTY. Hardly the stuff of mass unrest. But then few Americans understand what the Bank and the IMF actually do.

The two sister institutions, located across from each other on 19th Street, were created at the 1945 Bretton Woods conference—the Bank to lend money for development, the Fund to provide short-term liquidity loans to governments. The mission of the IMF, especially, has expanded greatly since then. It now oversees long-term reform in some 70-odd developing nations, assuming so instrumental a role in those countries' everyday affairs as to border on a shadow government. The comings and goings of IMF officials are frequently headline news.

The IMF's pitch to developing countries is basically this: We'll offer you x billion dollars, but only if you hew to a strict set of conditions—balanced budgets, low tariffs, free capital movements, deregulated labor markets, privatization, abolition of subsidies, and the rest of the neoliberal package that the *Times'* Friedman has aptly dubbed the "Golden Straitjacket." The theory: Reform yourselves to look like an open, Western economy, and GDP growth will follow in the long run. The short-term reality: austerity programs that often require deep cuts in health, education, and other basic spending.

Countries are nominally free to decline these loans, of course. But brush off the IMF, and private lenders and investors won't be knocking on your door anytime soon. "The IMF gets its way," writes Sachs, "because to disagree publicly with the IMF is viewed in the international community as rejecting financial rectitude itself."

The protesters accuse the U.S. of using the IMF as a stalking-horse to foist its brand of unfettered capitalism on the rest of the world.

So to whom does this immensely powerful institution answer? The IMF will tell you it's accountable to its 182 member governments, which is true. But voting is weighted by financial contribution, meaning the wealthy G-7 countries collectively control 45% of the voting power; India, home to one-sixth of the world's population, controls 2%. Not that the IMF holds many votes, anyway. Most of its deliberations, including the selection of its managing director, are conducted behind closed doors.

The protesters accuse the U.S. of using the IMF as a stalking-horse to foist its brand of unfettered capitalism on the rest of the world—a charge the cognoscenti dismiss as the rantings of economic illiterates and "one-world paranoids." But in March the Meltzer Commission, appointed by the Republican Congress to recommend IMF reforms, delivered the following assessment: "The G-7 governments, particularly the United States, use the IMF as a vehicle to achieve their political ends. This practice subverts democratic processes of creditor countries." If this statement raises a question, few in the press are asking it.

If the opacity of the IMF isn't enough to warrant closer inspection, its economic policies would seem to be. They have frequently proven ineffective, and occasionally disastrous. The Meltzer Commission could hardly have been blunter on this point: "Numerous studies of the effects of IMF lending have failed to find any significant link between IMF involvement and increases in wealth or income.

IMF-assisted bailouts of creditors in recent crises have had especially harsh effects on developing countries. People who have worked hard to struggle out of poverty have seen their achievements destroyed, their wealth and savings lost, and their small businesses bankrupted." A Jamaican cabdriver in D.C. concurred: "The IMF holds the haft of the sword," he said, "while the rest of the world holds the blade."

The IMF's biggest test case to date was the Asian financial crisis of 1997. The IMF points to Asia's subsequent rebound as proof of the efficacy of its intervention, blaming the crisis on "crony capitalism." And Friedman, in his best-selling book about globalization, *The Lexus and the Olive Tree,* takes that argument a step further: "I believe globalization did us all a favor by melting down the economies of Thailand, Korea, Malaysia, Indonesia, Mexico, Russia, and Brazil in the 1990s, because it laid bare a lot of rotten practices and institutions," he writes. "Exposing the crony capitalism in Korea was no crisis in my book."

But a very different story has emerged from such critics as Joseph Stiglitz, the former chief economist of the World Bank. As Stiglitz and others tell it, the roots of the crisis lay not in "crony capitalism" at all (indeed, Paul Volcker has noted that Asia grew quite handsomely for decades with its crony capitalism very much in place), but rather in a common result of economic liberalization: a flood of speculative, short-term capital that caused a real estate bubble in Thailand, then flooded out once the bubble burst. In other words, Stiglitz says the problem wasn't lack of openness but too much of it too soon. And who had pressured these countries to fling open their capital markets so precipitately? The U.S. Treasury and the IMF.

Though the point was often overlooked as capital rushed for the exits in Asia, it's worth remembering that countries like Taiwan and South Korea at the time still boasted sound fundamentals—budget surpluses, low inflation, high savings rates. No one disagrees that something had to be done to calm jittery creditors, but respected skeptics like Sachs maintain that the IMF's actions made a very bad situation worse. Its pronouncements that immediate surgery was needed, coupled with its Draconian prescriptions—bank closures, budget cuts, higher interest rates, and structural reforms intended to root out everything "wrong" with the Asian brand of capitalism—had an excessively deflationary effect, Sachs insists. "Instead of dousing the fire," he writes, "the IMF in effect screamed 'Fire!' in the theater." Stiglitz agrees that he, too, was "appalled."

The Asian economies recovered, but not before millions were reduced to the poverty many of them had so recently escaped. (And not before Malaysia flouted the IMF's advice by imposing capital controls that, shockingly, failed to bring about the predicted calamity.) More important, the critics complain that, in every crisis, whether in Africa or Latin America or Russia, the IMF deploys the same cookie-cutter policies. Stiglitz claims the economists who designed them "are more likely to have firsthand knowledge of [a country's] five-star hotels than of the villages that dot its countryside."

The World Bank has come in for similar abuse from a broad spectrum of opinion. What's under attack is a culture that rewards loan-making for its own sake, solicits little input from the local citizenry, favors huge infrastructure projects over direct poverty alleviation, and ignores the often devastating effects of its projects (the Sardar Sarovar Dam in India, to name but one horror story, threatens to displace a million or so people). But numbers speak loudest: By the Bank's own reckoning, nearly 60% of its projects are failures. In Africa, its track record is virtually unblemished by success.

> *Even granting the IMF's and World Bank's flaws, would the global economy really be better off if these institutions didn't exist?*

Of course, everyone's record in Africa is abysmal, from the most earnest nongovernment organizations on up. And therein lies the dilemma. It's easy for Seattle Man or Stiglitz (or me, for that matter) to pile on and blame the World Bank and the IMF for holding out the sword blade-first. But how else to hold it? The issues here are fearsomely complex. But alternatives do exist. Take the fundamental question: Even granting the IMF's and World Bank's flaws, would the global economy really be better off if these institutions didn't exist? Well, at least one distinguished (and mainstream) group, the Meltzer Commission, has essentially said yes. In its reform proposals, the commission calls for getting the IMF out of the nanny business and limiting itself to emergency lending during currency crises. It would also shift the World Bank's focus away from lending toward development assistance.

Even if the Bank and IMF stayed exactly as they are, they could stand a little structural adjustment of their own. Unlike your average elitist CEO, for example, most of these officials have never had to answer to anyone, least of all to a posse of angry shareholders or boycotting consumers or Greenpeace activists. Their insularity has bred, if not contempt, a palpable measure of obliviousness.

Which brings us to the third leg of what the protesters insist on calling the Iron Triangle of globalization: the World Trade Organization, object of last fall's Seattle ruckus. Based in Geneva, the

WTO wields far less power than the World Bank or the IMF. Yet its single-minded focus on flattening trade barriers obscures the fact that some basic economic differences are rooted in national choices about how to organize a society or a culture—and are driven by local politics. Who makes the decision when those choices don't square with the appetites of the global technocracy? Indeed many of the strategies pursued by the U.S. and Japan early in their own developments—selective tariffs, a bit of industrial policy here and there—wouldn't be permitted under today's WTO regime, which tends to see just about everything as an impediment to trade. Nor are the rich nations above occasionally rigging the game in their own favor. A tax holiday for America's fledgling e-commerce industry is all fine and good, but an African nation looking to protect its fledgling manufacturers—now that's antitrade, isn't it?

Taken together, these problems point to a looming democratic crisis of sorts. As Friedman argues in his book, decision-making is migrating to the international level, effectively stripping nation-states of some of their sovereignty. That in itself may not be a bad thing, but unlike national governments, these global institutions aren't bound by a broader system of checks and balances. In the meantime, there is literally no forum where representatives for workers, communities, human rights, or the environment can make their case at the global level with any hope of being heard. Except, of course, the streets.

"Aspiring business people shouldn't be protesting against imperialism. . . . It's a conflict of interest."—Paul Paftinos, a George Washington Univeristy student.

Out in said streets, I ran into a business student from George Washington University named Paul Paftinos. We were watching 600 protesters being rounded up, bound with yellow plastic cuffs, and shepherded onto a fleet of school buses. Paftinos noted disapprovingly that some of his fellow students might have been among them. "Aspiring business people shouldn't be protesting against imperialism," he said, with all apparent sincerity. "It's a conflict of interest."

Vivek Maru, a protester and second-year student at Yale Law School, seemed untroubled by such conflicts. He was wearing a Salomon Brothers jacket, the relic of a summer internship. "We're trying with voices and bodies to narrow this disjunct between abstract economic theories and real people on the ground. We're here standing against Fukuyama's 'End of History,'" he said, invoking the 1989 article that famously announced the world's convergence on a single model of democratic capitalism. "Alternatives are being extinguished. . . . But this is not the end."

Many doubt that such pleadings—or less reasoned ones, like the words SUCK IT, IMF! scrawled on 19th Street—can make much of a difference. The response to the spectacle of Gordon Brown, Britain's Chancellor of the Exchequer and thus a major player in the IMF, wasn't exactly encouraging: "Well, we didn't hear the protesters, and the meeting went on as normal; it started on time, and it was completed in the normal way."

And the sit-down-and-shut-up crowd does hold one final trump card. It's a cry that has become the 21st century's equivalent of waving the bloody shirt: "Protectionism!" There's not much to say to this, other than to observe that globalization's boosters seem to have become so besotted by its benefits, so forgetful that it creates both winners and losers, so intent on speechifying about the "power of the American idea," that they're at risk of becoming every bit as knee-jerk and blinkered as the most rabid protectionist. As Edward Luttwak, a senior fellow at the Center for Strategic and International Studies in Washington, quips: "The last time there was a group on the world scene who were this convinced they were completely right, it was the Bolsheviks."

The point is not that global integration is a bad thing. The point is that there is, or should be, a discussion here. It's not about free trade vs. protectionism, or capitalism vs. socialism, or anything easily reducible to a bumper sticker. Rather, the new debates will be about different variants of capitalism; about how much power nations should cede to the global marketplace; about the extent to which an economy should sustain a society, as opposed to the reverse. They'll be about the tradeoffs between economic security and economic efficiency, between growth and equality. And let's not forget: We do have a choice in these matters. New technologies will continue to make the world a smaller place no matter what, but economic integration is still very much driven by discrete political decisions. "The rules are not predetermined," says Harvard economist Dani Rodrik. "Globalization is not something that's just falling into our laps from another planet."

The wackos in the streets in Seattle and D.C. have caught on to this. Yes, their kind of protest is an ugly, untidy form of social change. It forces us to deal with women with foam trees on their heads. Many will find this lamentable. As Jesse Helms is supposed to have said once, "Democracy used to be a good thing, but now it has gotten into the hands of the wrong people." But it's time the empty cheerleading stopped. Else we might wake up one day to find that the cherished Washington Consensus has become a consensus of one.

The Other World Wide Web[4]

Global Public Policy Networks

By WOLFGANG H. REINICKE
FOREIGN POLICY, WINTER 1999/2000

Whining is a central feature of the debate on how best to meet the challenges of globalization. Traditional political institutions, we are told, are ever less capable of dealing with all the problems that lie ahead. The nation-state? Passé. International organizations? A story of failure rather than success. There are few newspaper or journal contributions that do not leave us with a certain sense of helplessness. Is this a form of millennial depression?

By concentrating on these old and well-worn stories, we may be missing a quiet revolution. Equating political change with political institutions masks a simple truth: Individuals and groups, not bureaucracies or formal institutions, drive innovation and learning. Change is a bottom-up process, not a top-down steering committee.

The advent of global public policy networks is a case in point. These networks are loose alliances of government agencies, international organizations, corporations, and elements of civil society such as nongovernmental organizations, professional associations, or religious groups that join together to achieve what none can accomplish on its own. Surveys by the World Bank in 1999 identified some 50 different global public policy networks, ranging in focus from crime to fisheries and public health. From the World Commission on Dams to the Roll Back Malaria initiative, these mostly new groupings thrive in a borderless environment and capitalize on technological innovation—the very conditions that hamper policy makers in traditional institutions. Perhaps most important, global public policy networks give once ignored groups from civil society a greater voice, thus narrowing the participatory gap and "democratic deficit" for which international decision making is often criticized. Although their objectives and budgets are still relatively modest, their record of success holds the promise not only of untangling a knot of global problems, but of improving the principles and methods of global governance.

---

4.   Article by Wofgang Reinecke from *Foreign Policy,* Winter 1999/2000. Copyright © Carnegie Endowment for the International Peace. Reprinted with permission.

Bureaucratic Growing Pains

Most global public policy networks have emerged over the last decade, experimenting with new ways to gather knowledge and disseminate information on specific issues. As public policy becomes increasingly influenced by global conditions, formal policy-making institutions—national legislatures, government agencies, and multilateral institutions, among others—often lack the scope, speed, and contacts to acquire and use crucial information needed to formulate effective policy.

First, growing social and economic integration around the world has extended the geographic scope of public policy far beyond national borders. As a result, decision makers must struggle to understand and respond to complex new challenges whose origins may lie far beyond their jurisdictions. The environmental arena offers some classic instances. For example, the release of chlorofluorocarbons in any one nation contributes to ozone depletion and ultimately to global warming, which affects all countries. Trapped by the territoriality of their power, policy makers in traditional settings often have little choice but to address the symptoms rather than the causes of public problems.

Second, the frenetic pace of technological change has drastically reduced the amount of time that policy makers have to develop new competencies or make key decisions. Regulators often find themselves playing "catch up" with the private sector, placing a premium on timely information about new developments in the markets they oversee. Recall the sudden and precipitous collapse of the Barings Group, a major U.K. bank, in early 1995. A once venerable financial institution, Barings was crippled by a lone trader's gamble on the direction of Japanese stock prices and interest rates. Yet financial regulators—traditionally focused on credit risk—were ill-equipped to assess or cope with the potential downside of technological advances in the financial services industry. In particular, regulators did not foresee how the use of innovative products such as derivatives—financial instruments whose value reflects that of other underlying assets—could lead to the abrupt Barings debacle.

Third, in addition to geographic and time constraints, policy makers must tackle more and more issues that cut across areas of bureaucratic or disciplinary expertise. An issue such as international trade policy can have profound economic, ecological, and security effects, all of which must be considered in the course of a policy debate. Although the intersection between international trade and domestic labor concerns, for example, is widely acknowledged, it remains highly contentious. Consider the bitter debates over the North American Free Trade Agreement in the early 1990s. Who had the expertise to develop policy dealing with international trade and workers' rights? The Mexican Congress? The Office of the U.S. Trade Representative? The International Labour Organization? None of the above? Reactions to the recent World Trade Organization meeting in Seattle only emphasize the extent to which trade policy has become a lightning rod for issues ranging from human rights to environmental degradation. This broadening of policy debates challenges the focus and structure of typical national or multilateral bureaucracies.

Network Solutions

Global public policy networks are helping policy makers meet these new challenges. Their broad membership allows them to tap information and expertise from a variety of backgrounds, providing them with a more complete picture of particular policy issues and

Growing social and economic integration around the world has extended the geographic scope of public policy far beyond national borders.

giving voice to previously unheard groups. By connecting groups that might not otherwise deal with one another, they also promote learning and collaboration. Health workers at a Peruvian NGO, World Bank consultants in Washington, researchers at a private French laboratory--each may hold part of an innovative mechanism to prevent cholera outbreaks. Global public policy networks help bring them together. Moreover, the networks' typically nonhierarchical organization allows them to acquire, process, and disseminate new knowledge more rapidly than mainstream policy bureaucracies. These characteristics give networks a particular advantage in three essential areas of global policy making: managing knowledge, overcoming market and intergovernmental coordination failures, and broadening participation.

Managing Knowledge

Global public policy networks have already proved their importance by consolidating relevant knowledge and disseminating it on a global scale. Consider the Consultative Group on International Agricultural Research (CGIAR). One of the oldest (founded in 1971) and most respected global policy networks, the CGIAR coordinates and helps finance the work of 16 independent agricultural research centers around the world. Its members meet twice a year to exchange views and discuss research agendas. Over the years, the centers forming part of this network have produced ground-breaking agricultural innovations. The International Rice Research Institute in the Philippines, for example, began to develop a new rice plant in 1989 that is expected to far surpass the typical production plateaus of even today's high-yield varieties. Currently undergoing further refinements, this "super rice" is expected to be in the fields by 2003. Other global public policy networks fulfilling similar roles in their respective fields include the Global Water Partnership—a network made up of governments, multilateral agencies, development banks, NGOs, and research organizations seeking to promote sustainable water management practices—and the Clean Air Initiative in Latin America.

But when public policy outcomes are at stake, agreeing on the "correct" knowledge can be a messy business. Financial regulation, environmental protection, and public health standards, for instance, have all become matters of significant transnational debate. A global public policy network can sort through conflicting perspectives, help hammer out a consensus, and translate that consensus into actions its members will be more inclined to support and implement. The value of a consensus-building network rests not on its ability to offer quick solutions, but on its creation of an environment that enables parties in conflict to reach an eventual agreement. Often such networks arise out of a crisis or stalemate, when those in conflict realize that no group can resolve the issue alone. The World Commission on Dams is a good example.

In the early 1990s, the construction of dams became one of the most conflict-ridden issues in the development community. The breakdown of dialogue between NGOs, the private sector, and international organizations such as the World Bank was imposing considerable costs on all parties. Dam construction contracts for private developers were drying up, NGOs were devoting considerable resources to sustain campaigns against large dams, and the World Bank was facing increasing difficulty in supporting related loans in the face of growing public pressure. This set of circumstances prompted the World Conservation Union (an environmental policy network made up of scientists, governments, and NGOs) and a small group of World Bank staff to experiment with a more inclusive forum for negotiations. An informal workshop in 1997 brought champions and critics of large dams together for an initial dialogue. A year later, the World Commission on Dams (WCD) was born. The WCD has a two-year mandate ending in June 2000 to spur the development of new standards for dam construction worldwide. To fulfill this goal, the commission is compiling detailed case studies of

15 large dams from Norway to Pakistan to South Africa to the United States and is assessing their performance and impact on local and regional development. A broader survey of 150 dams is also in the works. The commission has conducted regional consultations in Brazil and Sri Lanka to solicit feedback on dams from interested groups and individuals. All significant aspects of the WCD (membership, structure, and finance) are trisectoral in nature—that is, they involve governments, international organizations, and private groups. Although many observers doubted that the commission's work would extend beyond one meeting, today the WCD is recognized as an innovative response to a thorny global policy issue.

Correcting Market and Intergovernmental Failures

Trisectoral networks also provide a valuable public service by supporting the creation and deepening of markets that would otherwise likely not develop and by remedying the weaknesses and failures of existing private and public arrangements. Microlending networks, for example, help correct credit market failures by documenting and disseminating best practices on lending to the poor. The Microcredit Summit, held in Washington, D.C., in early 1997, brought together some 2,900 people from 137 countries and 1,500 organizations to discuss mechanisms for expanding credit for self-employment and other financial and business services to the world's poorest families. The meeting also launched an ambitious "global fulfillment campaign" to provide an additional 100 million poor families with access to credit by 2005. To promote the exchange of best practices, the network has established "microcredit summit councils" for different sectors, including international financial institutions, NGOs, governments, and educational and religious organizations.

Similarly, the Global Reporting Initiative (GRI)—a network connecting environmental NGOs, private firms, governments, and professional associations—is helping develop uniform standards for assessing the environmental impact of private corporations. Although many firms are voluntarily producing and releasing such assessments, each employs its own indicators and measurements, making it virtually impossible for investors, environmentalists, or consumers to compare reports and make informed decisions. Established in 1997, the GRI plans to complete its "corporate environmental sustainability" guidelines by the end of 1999.

Global public policy networks can also help implement existing international accords. The Global Environment Facility (GEF), for example, provides grants and concessional financing for environmental projects in countries seeking to adhere to international treaties on climate change, biological diversity, and ozone depletion. It also administers a small grants program for projects by NGOs and community groups. Since 1991, the GEF has funded approximately 500 projects in 120 countries, disbursing more than $2 billion in financing. Funds provided by GEF have promoted the development of solar energy use in Argentina, the construction of port waste facilities in eastern Caribbean countries, and the protection of Indonesia's coral reefs. Additional cofinancing for GEF projects has reached $5 billion, with 40 percent coming from recipient countries. Administered by the World Bank, the U.N. Development Programme, and the U.N. Environment Programme, the GEF is governed by a council of 18 recipient and 14 nonrecipient nations.

The Roll Back Malaria (RBM) initiative, a policy network spearheaded by the World Health Organization (WHO), is seeking to overcome decades of limited financing and poor implementation in the fight against malaria, particularly in Africa. According to the WHO, most victims of the disease die because of poor access to health services or simply because of inadequate precautionary measures. Only a year old, the initiative is establishing partnerships among government agencies, multilateral organizations, NGOs, and the private sector to upgrade health services, intensify the use of bednetting (nets coated with insecticides), and develop vaccines as well as new drugs for those who are already infected. Although such efforts primarily appear to help developing countries, advanced nations will also benefit from greater control over malaria. As global trade brings countries closer together, diseases will tend not to discriminate according to a country's per capita income. (A Centers for Disease Control and Prevention official was recently quoted as saying there is "no question" that malaria will penetrate the United States in the next decade.) Though it is too early to assess its full impact, the RBM represents a trisectoral effort to correct a recurrent multilateral failure.

Broadening Participation

Ultimately, trisectoral networks embody an effort to determine what is in the global public interest and how it can be achieved effectively and efficiently. To reach such a consensus, successful global public policy networks bring together groups that often work at cross purposes—typically, the NGO community versus multilateral organizations or the private sector versus government. The networks' inclusiveness lends legitimacy to ensuing policy discussions and increases the likelihood that all parties will accept the outcomes. The Global Water Partnership (GWP), for example, has created regional advisory committees in seven countries so that local organizations can contribute to the sharing of best practices on water management. For global public policy networks to maintain their credibility, broad participation is important not only in membership but in financing and structure as well. The World Commission on Dams provides a strong example of participatory practices: Its members share funding responsibilities, and all sectors participated in formulating the network's mandate and selecting its leadership.

Support Your Local Network

Global governance is not a zero-sum game. Embracing global public policy networks does not imply a "power shift" away from governments and international organizations toward civil society and the private sector. Trisectoral networks are meant to complement traditional public policy institutions, not replace them. They help governments and multilateral agencies to manage risks, take advantage of opportunities presented by technological change, be more responsive to their constituents, and promote change within bureaucracies. New networks may also emerge to help traditional policy makers address cutting-edge global challenges, such as transnational crime, money laundering, and the furious debate over biotechnology and genetically modified foods.

Mindful of these benefits, governments are throwing more weight behind global public policy networks. Led by Germany and Norway, national governments account for 40 percent of funding for the World Commission on Dams. A number of Organisation for Economic Cooperation and Development countries strongly support the development of new vaccines for malaria and other diseases. The Swedish International Development Cooperation Agency is among the principal sponsors of the Global Water Partnership, while the member states of the Association of Southeast Asian Nations support a regional GWP network.

Multilateral organizations in particular recognize that global public policy networks provide them with the ideal means through which to reposition themselves and sharpen their missions. U.N. Secretary General Kofi Annan has expressed strong support for such initiatives, and World Bank President James Wolfensohn has made connecting "coalitions for change" an explicit priority of his second term.

From the networks' perspective, multilateral organizations are a crucial source of support. The World Health Organization played a central role in the development of the Roll Back Malaria initiative, and both the Global Water Partnership and the World Commission on Dams received strong early backing from the World Bank. The global reach and knowledge of international organizations provide a solid foundation for them to convene and facilitate new networks. Less than 10 years old in most cases, global public policy networks remain in relative infancy. They need the institutional and personal leadership that international organizations can provide.

But leadership, individual and institutional alike, can also turn into a liability. Once a network has passed the early hurdles and established itself as a powerful voice on a particular global issue, its founders must be ready to step back and recruit constituents from other sectors for leadership roles. This form of "leading from behind" has proved successful. Both the World Conservation Union and the World Bank pared back their involvement in the World Commission on Dams after its inception, thereby solidifying the network's perceived legitimacy and impartiality.

> *Global governance is not a zero-sum game.*

The roles of individuals and organizations in a network can change over time. Indeed, there is good reason to believe that both the World Conservation Union and the World Bank will again become formally involved once implementation of the WCD's dam construction standards becomes the network's principal task.

Given the demonstrated contributions of global public policy networks, governments and international organizations share an interest in ensuring their long-term financial support and in providing the seed money needed to get a network off the ground. Although such initial funding often comes from a single source, more varied sources of financial support are especially important when the network's primary purpose is to build consensus around a policy issue. To preserve the WCD's credibility, its funding is distributed among government agencies, multilateral organizations, the private corporations, and NGOs and foundations. Such strict funding arrangements are less crucial for networks focused on policy implementation. The Global Environment Facility, mainly a financing mechanism supporting intergovernmental treaties, is funded entirely by governments. Given the GEF's mandate, this single source does not undermine the network's standing.

The Strength of Weak Ties

Economic sociologist Mark Granovetter suggested more than 25 years ago that "those to whom we are weakly tied are more likely to move in circles different from our own and will thus have access to information different from that which we receive." Acquiring information from geographically distant and culturally diverse sources is not just politically correct handwringing—it is a key advantage in global public policy making. Through the "strength of weak ties," networks take maximum advantage of the tensions and differences among disparate groups. Though trisectoral networks are no panacea for all global problems—some millennial depression may yet be warranted—their emergence could represent the early skirmishes of a revolution in global public policy making.

Unfortunately, although inclusiveness may be these networks' greatest contribution to global public policy, the mere facade of inclusiveness may prove their fatal weakness. It should come as no surprise that there is a tendency for Western governments, large multinational corporations, and prominent NGOs to dominate these networks. And though their presence may fulfill the "trisectoral" requirement of a global public policy network, this dominance means that many voices remain silent. To ensure their success, global public policy networks must indeed be global. The inclusion of less powerful yet important groups from the developing world is critical not just for designing policies but even more so for implementing them. Central governments, for example, should encourage state and local leaders—the ones likely to be involved in seeing policies through—to join the debate. A lesser-known NGO in a poor nation may hold the key to solving an ancient economic or environmental puzzle. Will we ever know? Unless global public policy networks constantly bolster their ranks with new voices, they risk becoming as sluggish as the traditional bureaucracies they now seek to help.

A NETWORK SAMPLER

ROLL BACK MALARIA

Founding Date: 1998
Objective: To reduce malaria-related mortality rates, particularly in Africa, and to help improve affected countries' health systems.
Membership: The World Health Organization, World Bank, UNICEF, UNDP, government agencies, development banks, bilateral agencies, private sector bodies, and NGOs.
Budget and Funding: $20.1 million in 1999.

THE CONSULTATIVE GROUP ON INTERNATIONAL AGRICULTURAL RESEARCH

Founding Date: 1971
Objective: To promote food security through innovative and sustainable agricultural practices.
Membership: 58 members, including 21 developed and 20 developing nations, foundations, and international or regional organizations. Partner organizations include NGOs and private corporations.
Budget and Funding: $345 million in 1998. Industrial countries, specifically the members of the OECD's Development Assistance Committee, account for more than two thirds of CGIAR financing.

THE GLOBAL ENVIRONMENT FACILITY

Founding Date: 1991
Objective: To finance environmental projects for recipient governments and NGOs seeking to promote biodiversity, improve energy efficiency, reverse the degradation of international waters, and phase out the use of ozone-damaging substances.
Membership: 165 governments. The governing council is composed of 16 representatives from developing countries, 14 from developed nations, and 2 from transition economies.
Budget and Funding: $2 billion pledged toward its trust fund in 1994. An additional $2.75 billion was added in 1998 by 36 developed, transition, and developing countries. GEF collaborates with the private sector to mobilize project cofinancing.

THE WORLD COMMISSION ON DAMS

Founding Date: 1998
Objective: To undertake a global review of the development effectiveness of large dams and establish internationally accepted criteria for dam construction.
Membership: Government agencies, multilateral development banks, bilateral agencies, domestic river basin authories, research institutes, hydropower companies, and NGOs representing persons affected by dam construction.

Budget and Funding: $9.8 million. Donations have come from member governments, the World Bank, World Conservation Union, NGOs such as the Worldwide Fund for Nature, foundations such as the U.N. Foundation, and private firms such as the ABB Group.

THE GLOBAL WATER PARTNERSHIP

Founding Date: 1996

Objective: To improve management of the world's water resources.

Membership: Governments of developing and developed countries, U.N. agencies, development banks, professional associations, research organizations, private corporations, and NGOs.

Budget and Funding: $6 million. Sponsors include the World Bank, Swedish International Development Cooperation Agency, and UNDP. The Ford Foundation and several Western European governments provide additional support.

The Godfathers Go Global[5]

BY JOHN LLOYD
NEW STATESMAN, DECEMBER 20, 1999

In the summer of 1992, a group of killers sat on a hillside in Capaci, Sicily, smoking and watching the motorway below. When two cars in tight formation appeared, one of the men threw a switch: the road under the cars exploded. The bomb blast killed the magistrate Giovanni Falcone, his wife and three police officers who were guarding him.

The police who came to the crime scene were drawn from the Italian police forces—and from the FBI. They found the cigarette butts that the assassins had dropped. The butts were taken to a FBI laboratory, examined by Italian officers—and the DNA scraped off the butts finally identified the killers who came to trial and were sentenced, five years later. It is an encouraging story; something of a recompense for the murder of a man who, more than any other, epitomised the struggle of the Italian state with organised crime in its very heartland. The co-operation had its origin in meetings a decade before Falcone's death, when Italian and U.S. police agencies decided to attack their common—and increasingly linked—Mafia problem together.

International co-operation on combating organised crime has greatly increased: the FBI, once almost exclusively a domestic agency, now has around three hundred "legates" or officers posted abroad in U.S. embassies and it co-operates directly with police forces in over 30 countries. Yet the links formed between the law are nothing compared to the growth of organised crime over the past decade. It is the greatest success story of the end of the 20th century.

"Organised crime," says Professor Louise Shelley of Washington's American University, "will be a defining issue of the 21st century as the cold war was for the 20th century and colonialism was for the 19th century. Transnational crime will proliferate because crime groups are the major beneficiaries of globalisation."

The freedoms of the post-cold-war era have come too quickly for law and order. The collapse of authoritarian regimes in the east has not been followed by a building of democratic order: on the contrary, in many of the societies of the former Soviet Union—including the two largest, Russia and Ukraine—the state has little effective power to enforce the law and has very substantially merged with criminal and corrupt interests. Russia has between five and six thousand organised crime gangs with 100,000 members, the most active and ruthless of these operating increasingly abroad.

"It is clear," says Phil Williams, an American expert on organised crime, "that the Chinese Triad, Russian criminal organisations, Colombian cartels, Japanese yakuza, Sicilian Mafia as well as other Italian groups such as the Neapolitan Camorra, 'Ndrangheta and the Sacra Corona Unita, Nigerian criminal organisations and Turkish drug-trafficking groups engage in extensive criminal activities on a regional, and often global, basis. These organisations violate national sovereignty, undermine democratic institutions even in states where these institutions are well established, threaten the process of democratisation and privatisation in states in transition and add a new dimension to problems such as nuclear proliferation and terrorism."

Their global reach was illustrated early in December, when Edmond Safra, one of the world's 200 richest men and owner of the private Republic National Bank of New York, was murdered in his flat in Monaco. The immediate speculation was that his assassins were Russian contract killers: his bank was answering questions on money laundering and, according to one anonymous friend, his family believes "someone decided to send a message to the bank not to co-operate." Safra was well guarded, in a flat built for protection; he numbered heads of state among his friends: that he should be so contemptuously taken out shows the sense of power now enjoyed by the crime bosses—as well as the height of the stakes for which they play.

The global drug industry alone now accounts for 2 per cent of the world economy—and rising. It is both very powerful and very flexible. When the FBI succeeded in closing down the conduit for drugs from Colombia through the Caribbean to the U.S., the Colombians rapidly opened up a new corridor—through Mexico, where the organised crime problem is rising exponentially.

But drugs may not be the largest part of the global mafia's business. Jack Blum, a Washington lawyer and Senate investigator of organised crime, said in testimony to a Congressional committee last year that "fraud of various kinds is, in terms of its social implications, the most dangerous of all. Mafia-related stock fraud uses offshore corporations, using various hideouts in the international system to manipulate stock-market prices and take advantage of investors in the US. The problem is, who has the authority to investigate? Whose job is it to police the international financial system? And, in the end, how will you ever bring any of the perpetrators to justice or recover any of the money?"

Blum's point is given extra force by the loopholes in the world economy, which leave plenty of room for organised crime to flourish. There are now around 50 "states" in the world that exist largely by selling their national sovereignty to those who wish to buy it in order to make their business deals inconspicuous. The "state" of Dominica advertises itself on the World Wide Web—its passport can be bought in a package with a name change, under the slogan "Perfect for someone who would like to leave his past behind." There is no mystery as to what these states do: but since they have the formal attributes of independent states, they cannot simply be closed down.

The free-doms of the post-cold-war era have come too quickly for law and order.

Globalisation has another, seamier downside. As developing world cities proliferate and local customs and inhibitions break down, slavery—especially sex slavery—is growing rapidly, a trade also commanded by organised crime. At the more "sophisticated" end of the market, this can be an international trade, with brothels set up or supplied all over the world: more frequently, it is the induction of girls, often no more than children, into a world where they are brutalised both by their clients and pimps. It is also a world that lives cheek by jowl with the advanced economy: Edward Luttwak, the U.S. analyst who has a dystopian vision of what he calls "turbo capitalism," writes that in Pakistan, "within walking distance of law courts, police stations, universities and computer software outfits satellite linked with Silicon Valley, young girls are brought each day from villages far and near to live in slavery, after being inducted into the trade by rape and beatings."

Modernisation proceeds unevenly, and for ill as well as for good. The sheer profusion of people in many parts of the world means that life is, literally, regarded as cheap: and the more ambitious seek work as the foot soldiers of organised crime, just as the Sicilian peasants of the 19th and early 20th centuries sought the protection and rewards of the gang—whether in Palermo or New York. But now there are many more foot soldiers and the gangs are huge—and globally organised. In November this year, Tony Blair called in the heads of the three main security agencies—Stephen Lander of MI5, Richard Dearlove of MI6 and Francis Richards of the GCHQ signal intelligence agency—for a meeting in Downing Street. The three directors told the Prime Minister that organised crime was now the largest threat to national security.

Blair is since reported to have told colleagues that he believed that, by boosting crimes of all kinds, the global mafia could threaten Labour's election chances.

The directors told Blair that there were five "fever spots." First and most serious were the former Soviet mafias—more ruthless, hungrier and greedier than any other, whose work includes contract killing and sophisticated computer fraud. Albania's collapse as a state released gangs that traffic in prostitution and arms—with links to the growing Albanian communities all over Europe. Turkey's drug gangs are now among the most active in the world: they told the Prime Minister that four-fifths of the heroin in Britain came from Turkish sources. West African gangs are becoming increasingly expert in credit-card and welfare fraud. Cigarette smuggling by Asian gangs is estimated to be worth £1.7 billion a year. These gangs are largely new, or rapidly growing, and are in addition to the more established Sicilian, Triad and other networks, with which they compete or co-operate. In response, the government is to pump more money into these agencies' surveillance of the criminal networks. Yet the kind of stateless space in which these criminals operate will prove very hard to police.

The sheer profusion of people in many parts of the world means that life is, literally, regarded as cheap.

The sheer range of the criminal links is breathtaking. In 1993, U.S. border police arrested around five hundred Chinese coming over the border between Mexico and the U.S. through what the *Los Angeles Times* called "a clandestine corridor linking the villages of Fujuian, the shores of Mexico and Central America and suburban safe houses in the heavily Chinese enclaves of the San Gabriel Valley." The example showed that Chinese, Central American and Mexican gangs could co-operate successfully in a human smuggling operation across thousands of miles. It also showed that a globalised world is one where the poor of the Earth are no longer resigned to their fate. The end of the century has seen the death of stoicism and fatalism. Like westerners, people of the developing world want to improve their lot: balked at home, they travel to richer places. "People no longer sit at home in poverty," says Marjorie Newman-Williams, a senior official of Unicef. "They get up and go. That's an attribute people in the west have been taught to admire."

This is a dark ending to a millennium whose brightness seemed so obvious a decade ago. It need not be for ever. Lawlessness has ruled large tracts of the earth for many periods of history: indeed, the relatively law-abiding developed states of the 20th century have been more exceptions than rules. They can deploy a battery of weapons. In the end, though, they must rely on freedom producing an antidote to licence: for the moment, it is fuelling it.

The Man from Interpol[6]

BY ALICE DRAGOON
CIO MAGAZINE, JUNE 15, 2000

He began his 30-year career in law enforcement as a bobby on the beat in London and once helped track down an IRA bomber. But today, Peter J. Nevitt fights crime on a global scale as director of IS at Interpol.

Despite its reputation, Interpol is not a secret organization of superspies and double agents. Rather, it's a network of 178 member countries whose police forces share leads and cooperate on international criminal investigations. Since 1923, Interpol has been helping the world's law enforcement officers track thieves, terrorists and other assorted thugs and bad guys.

Today, e-mail sent over secure networks has replaced Morse code as a means of information sharing, and Interpol maintains vast databases of wanted criminals, missing persons, organized crime groups, drug seizures, unidentified dead bodies and stolen artwork, to name a few. IT has become such a powerful weapon in the sometimes lengthy and complex pursuit of enemies of the global states that roughly 20 percent of Interpol's annual budget of $30 million is devoted to IT.

For Nevitt, who says he's long been interested in the application of technology in the police world, serving as Interpol's director of IS is "the ultimate techno-police officer's job." He recently spoke with Senior Editor Alice Dragoon from Interpol's headquarters in Lyon, France.

CIO: Many people who watched *The Man from U.N.C.L.E.* will be surprised to learn that Interpol isn't an international spy organization but actually a network that the world's law enforcement agencies use to share information.

Nevitt: Yes, we're seen as a semimythical organization of super-sleuths. We want to get rid of the myth; we're not interested in it. Well, we like it a little, of course, but the reality is better.

So set us straight: What really happens at Interpol?

6. Article by Alice Dragoon from *CIO Magazine,* June 15, 2000. Copyright © *CIO Magazine.* Reprinted with permission.

We have a network linking 178 countries and the Interpol general secretariat. Through that network, we offer two kinds of services. The first is an e-mail service. Country A sends a message to Country B asking for assistance or cooperation. Country B replies. During 1998, 2.4 million messages went through our network.

We also provide access to an international database of criminal information. So countries use e-mail to send information to the general secretariat, who incorporates it in the international database and then makes that database available to every country in the world or to those countries that the owner of the information authorizes.

How do you make information available to some countries but not to others?

We do it by the design of the system, which is based on tables. So if Country X has not been granted access to information from Country Y, and Country X does a search, the system will recognize that this information is denied and Country X won't know it's there.

> *Interpol is an organization of mutual cooperation, so it can't force any action.*

It's not just a question of diplomatic relationships either. Sometimes it's a question of trust or the need for secrecy among a small group of countries with a specific project. So a message can be one-to-one, one-to-several, one-to-many or one-to-all. And we can also do what we call a "full diffusion" of the message—such as a circulation of a wanted person—from the originating country to every country in the world in five minutes.

What happens once countries get these messages?

Interpol is an organization of mutual cooperation, so it can't force any action. It's the responsibility of each country within its own national laws to take whatever action is appropriate.

How was information stored and shared at Interpol before the advent of databases and e-mail?

Originally, information was stored in manual files in enormous archives down which clerks used to slide on chairs attached to rails. Not surprisingly, response times for queries were measured in days rather than seconds.

In the early 1980s, member countries communicated to Interpol and to one another through telex, Morse code and HF radio. Interpol also developed its own coded language for radio transmissions.

What would a typical message in that code have said?

You could use one word such as "alone," and it would translate as a phrase, such as "Please allow an officer to arrest this man." Or "bakle," which is used to describe a person in detention. It means "He's been placed in detention awaiting trial." I have operators working for me who still use this archaic language.

So how did Interpol move from the days of coded messages and Morse code into the IT era?

We began design of a global telecommunications network in the early '90s. In 1994, we began rolling it out to the world, an X.400 network running over X.25 lines. The rollout was finished only last year. The problem was that only one-quarter of the countries could afford the equipment and the line. So Interpol raised money from its richer members and from other organizations, such as the United Nations, to fund the leased lines, install the equipment and provide training in 130 of its 150 member countries. Interpol was one of the first major global organizations to contract with SITA, which is now Equant NV—a private company created and owned by a consortium of airline companies that collaborated to develop a global network for ticket reservations, air traffic control and so on—to act as network operator and to install and maintain the equipment.

Since the explosion of the Internet, how have you been using the Web?

Like most organizations, we're working out how we adapt to it. At the moment, we're using Internet technologies in three ways. The first is a public relations website. And here we're providing simple, nonsensitive police information—such as information on children or on what we're doing with counterfeit credit cards—directly to the public.

The criminal opportunities and the technologies are changing so fast that it's very difficult to stay at the leading edge.

The second is a secure domain of the site where we publish restricted information, which helps investigators do their jobs. For example, using counterfeit credit cards is an international criminal activity. We have developed a technique, not unlike fingerprint identification, that defines the characteristics of a genuine original and of a counterfeit. And we publish that information so that investigators of counterfeit credit card crimes have a database that they can use as a research tool.

The third way we're using Internet technologies is to replace our X.400 network with a secure IP network.

What do you do to ensure that your databases are secure?

We don't regard ourselves as the world's leading experts on security. The criminal opportunities and the technologies are changing so fast that it's very difficult to stay at the leading edge. So we are a member of the Information Security Forum, a cooperative group of some of the major European companies and government organizations that share expertise on security and develop and apply standards.

How would a police officer go about tapping into Interpol's databases of criminal information?

On a day-to-day basis, hundreds of searches are made of the international databases. Typically, a police officer or a customs officer at a port wants to check on a vehicle, so a search will be made on an Interpol database. As a result of introducing this international database of 2.3 million stolen motor vehicles, hundreds of those vehicles are identified and recovered every year.

Similarly, when police officers are checking individuals and think that there might be an international dimension to the check, they will consult the database to see whether they find a "hit" on that person—whether he or she is recorded as wanted in another country. It's a regular occurrence.

But the most interesting things, of course, are the international multicountry operations that may last for eons and have much more significant results.

Can you describe such an operation?

One that started about two and a half years ago involved heroin smuggled from Thailand in hollowed out books in a series titled "Show Me How." The investing action began with an inquiry from a U.K. agency asking if we had any records of drug seizures relating to small packages delivered to hotels. We searched our databases and found a few examples that had been reported to us. The examples were mainly in Europe, but all of them had a link to Bangkok— a parcel was posted in Bangkok to a European city close to an international airport, like Heathrow or Frankfurt Airport. That gave the investigator in the U.K. a lead for his inquiry and gave us an indication that this may be part of something bigger.

So we asked every country to search their national records and tell us whether they had examples of similar incidents that they had not reported. And within 24 hours, 50 countries—in Europe, Africa, Central America and North America—said they recently had such seizures.

We called a meeting in Lyon of the investigating officers from as many of these countries as we could get to come to Lyon—because face-to-face they will share information that they may not otherwise provide.

As a result of that, a multicountry operation coordinated by Interpol began to focus on these hotels in different countries. [The investigation led to the discovery of] Nigerian criminal gangs operating out of Bangkok and Bogota, Colombia. And so it was not just heroin from Bangkok, but opium and cocaine from Bogota. During the last two years, a significant number of arrests have been made in various countries on all continents, involving many seizures of heroin and opium. And a very important international gang of drug smugglers has been disrupted.

Moving from the seamy world of drug smuggling to the rarified air of art museums, doesn't Interpol also help countries recover stolen artwork?

We've got something like 15,000 or 16,000 items in the international database of stolen works of art. To identify a picture as identical to one that is stolen, police officers describe the unique characteristics of the item in lay terms (for example, painting size, internal or external scene, man seated, horse and water). The computer searches and provides pictures that seem to match. It is a very effective approach and requires no artistic expertise or knowledge. We also publish a CD-ROM with this information for national law enforcement agencies and for art dealers. So Christie's and Sotheby's and other art dealers have the Interpol database.

How would art dealers use that information?

Here's an example: An Italian art dealer went to do business with an art dealer in the United States and had this CD-ROM in his briefcase. The guy in the United States was talking about a bust that he had bought recently. He was very proud of it, and it was going to be auctioned. The Italian art dealer said, "Wouldn't it be interesting to see if it was in the Interpol database?" And he loaded his CD-ROM and bingo, there it was.

So the American art dealer went to the local police and said, "Look, I've bought this in good faith. It appears to be a stolen work of art." And the police then contacted their Interpol National Central Bureau, and the NCB contacted Interpol headquarters. We confirmed it with our works-of-art specialist, contacted the originating country and said, "Your bust is in New York with an art dealer." Then they entered the complex process of recovery. Eventually the piece was repatriated.

Interpol's mission is to track down some of the world's most unsavory characters. Have you been able to maintain faith in humanity while working there?

I can't think of a more exciting mission than to help make the world a safer and nicer place to live by providing these services to the police forces of the world. I think it's a great place to be.

IV. Culture Clash: Identical Ideologies or Ideological Identities?

Editor's Introduction

While many economists and politicians concern themselves with the economic and legal aspects of globalization, a growing number of academicians and protesters focus on globalization's influence on culture. As we saw in Juan Enriquez's "Too Many Flags" from Section I, countries often use culture to define themselves. Many people fear that a global society will produce a homogenous culture, one that does not allow for differences of taste, sight, sound, or tradition. In losing a culture, a society loses its identity, what makes it different from the rest of the world.

In the first article for this section, the author of an Associated Press article reprinted from the *New York Times* links language to the fate of culture. Focusing on tribes in the Amazon basin of South America, the author states that many of the traditional languages are kept alive by only a handful of people. Spanish and Portuguese, the languages of the conquistadors, was forcefully imposed on the speakers of the old languages, often the last remaining guardians of a past way of life.

In the essay "The World Gets in Touch with Its Inner American" (from *Mother Jones*), G. Pascal Zachary charges that the globalization of culture is nothing more than the Americanization of the world. He cites instances in Thailand, Malaysia, and France in which American goods supersede local products, and citizens of these countries prefer American products over their own. As further proof of Americanization, Zachary observes that the IMF, the fund created to hand out short-term loans to countries in need, often plays by rules dictated by the United States. As a result, he finds that resistance to America is rising, and he wonders whether or not America is exporting only the worst parts of its culture.

Erla Zwingle disagrees with Zachary. She writes in "A World Together," published in *National Geographic*, that while goods, people, and ideas have always moved, culture has always changed. Economic globalization has simply served to accelerate the process of cultural evolution. She identifies a variety of inroads into American culture in the United States, such as the current popularity of mehndi (a non-permanent form of tattoo painting) and mahjong on the Internet. She also points out that companies that go global in the overall scheme resort to going local in their new, foreign locales. In short, the spread of globalization heralds nothing more than a linking of cultures that will transform one another, rather than create a uniform culture.

This section concludes with an editorial from the *Far Eastern Economic Review* entitled "Global Culture." The author goes a step beyond the views expressed in the previous three articles to assert that globalization has extended beyond the simple exchange of cultural goods and fads. He declares that the way Westerners think, as exemplified by architectural methods, was imported by Asians some time ago. He suggests, therefore, that the criteria used by academicians and writers to prove the loss of individual cultures (the acceptance of fast food as epitomized by McDonald's and KFC, for example) are subjective. The lightbulb is a Western invention, but its use around the world is never descried as an abomination or used as a symbol of Westernization. This editorial questions the way we look at globalization, especially in regard to its influence on culture.

With World Opening Up, Languages Are Losers[1]

Anonymous
New York Times, May 16, 1999

As she tickles her two squealing grandchildren, the woman with the long gray hair forgets herself in her joy and begins speaking in her native Chamicuro tongue.

No one understands her. So Natalia Sangama wistfully switches to Spanish—now the language of her people, her children, her grandchildren.

"I dream in Chamicuro, but I cannot tell my dreams to anyone," the last fluent speaker of the language tells a reporter visiting her village, a cluster of thatch huts on the banks of a sky-blue lake in the Amazon jungle.

"Some things cannot be said in Spanish," Ms. Sangama said. "It's lonely being the last one."

Four other elderly inhabitants of Pampa Hermosa, 420 miles northeast of Lima, know bits and pieces of Chamicuro. But linguists say when Sangama dies, the language will die with her.

Many of the world's languages are disappearing as modern communications, migration and population growth end the isolation of ethnic groups. Linguists warn that one result is a "crash" in cultural and intellectual diversity similar to what many biologists say is happening in animal and plant species as wilderness areas are cleared.

Each language contains words that uniquely capture ideas, and when the words are lost, so are the ideas, linguists say.

At least half the world's 6,000 languages will probably die out in the next century and only 5 percent of languages are "safe," meaning they are spoken by at least a million people and receive state backing, experts say.

"There are hundreds of languages that are down to a few elderly speakers and are for the most part beyond hope of revival," said Doug Whalen, a Yale University linguist who is president of the Endangered Language Fund.

---

1. From the *New York Times,* May 16, 1999. Copyright © *New York Times.* Reprinted with permission.

The loss of languages is damaging because when a language dies much of a culture dies with it, said Michael Krauss, a University of Alaska linguist who compares linguistic diversity to biological diversity.

The human race evolved with a diversity of languages, which formed a rich pool of varied ideas and world views, but the pool is shrinking fast, he said. As contact between cultures has grown with globalization, the process of dominant languages killing off smaller languages has accelerated, he said.

"It's a cultural narrowing," Mr. Whalen said. "It may not be plagues and pestilence, but it is a cultural disaster."

The extinction process can best be seen in places like Peru's Amazon jungle, where some languages are still being discovered while others become extinct.

> *The human race evolved with a diversity of languages, which formed a rich pool of varied ideas and world views, but the pool is shrinking fast.*—**Michael Krauss, a University of Alaska linguist**

"South America has languages that are only now being discovered, and as soon as they are discovered they become endangered," Mr. Whalen said. "The mechanism of discovery immediately endangers them."

The Peruvian Amazon was called a Tower of Babel by early Spanish missionaries stunned by the number of languages they found among isolated communities separated by dense jungle.

Missionaries estimated that more than 500 languages were spoken in an area half the size of Alaska. Linguists now estimate there were probably 100-150 languages, but with a dizzying array of dialects.

Today, only 57 survive and 25 of them are on the road to extinction, said Mary Ruth Wise, a linguist with the Dallas-based Summer Institute of Linguistics.

In Pampa Hermosa, the last Chamicuros live without roads, electricity or telephones, the jungle looming around the village like a dense green wall. But a radio blares Spanish news and salsa music from a station in Yurimaguas, a town eight hours away by river boat.

Smallpox, migration and assimilation into the dominant Spanish culture have reduced the number of Chamicuros from 4,000 at the time of the Spanish conquest to 125 today. They live by fishing in dugout canoes carved from tree trunks, hunting and growing corn, yucca and beans.

"In the missionary school they used to make us kneel on corn if we spoke Chamicuro," Ms. Sangama recalled.

Farther along Lake Achual Tipishca live the Cocama-Cocamillas, a more numerous tribe of former headhunters who have also lost much of their culture to the dominant Spanish mestizo society.

Carlos Murayari, a 64-year-old river fisherman, has 11 children, but none speak Cocama-Cocamilla. "I tried to teach them Cocama-Cocamilla but Spanish took over," he said. "It's like paddling against the current."

Pulling flopping lake fish from his net, Mr. Murayari said he dreams of the "Land Without Evil," the Cocama-Cocamilla heaven that awaits people who have lived well. "Maybe there I won't be so alone," he said.

The World Gets in Touch with Its Inner American[2]

By G. Pascal Zachary
Mother Jones, January/February 1999

The woman sitting across from me in Bangkok's swank Dusit Thani hotel is one of Thailand's best and brightest. Educated in the U.S., she's a computer whiz at a prominent local company. She wears a basic business suit and impresses me with talk of "TCP/IP" and other Internet protocols. But when our conversation comes around to her romantic life, her fiancé—a New Yorker seated next to her—squirms. She admits it's a little odd not to be marrying a Thai. Still, she says in a low, conspiratorial voice, "Many Thai women dream of having an American's baby."

My jaw drops. I expect her to give her boyfriend, who works for a U.S. corporation here, a reassuring smile, as if to say that she isn't one of them. But she goes right on talking. "Thai people think these babies are more beautiful, better endowed," she says. "They're all the rage."

The Thai passion for Americana doesn't stop with babies. Thai consumers learned the concept of "nutritional value" labeling from Frito-Lay packages, the first in the nation to carry an analysis of potato chip ingredients. The government's response to its financial collapse, which triggered the Asian economic meltdown, "draws from the United States" handling of its S&L crisis in the 1980s. Thailand's largest private employer, Seagate Technology, is a U.S. high-tech company. And the country's new constitution retreats from Asian communalism by emphasizing a core American value: individual rights.

Others countries are following Thailand's lead. A few days before arriving in Bangkok, I listen to Ella Fitzgerald piped over a stereo system in a restaurant in Kuala Lumpur's trendy Bangsar district. I am eating a bowl of laksa, a traditional stew. My lunch companion is Karim Raslan, a lawyer and leading Malaysian social critic. Notoriously prickly about their own culture, Malaysians have criticized Americans for our unbridled individualism. Yet in the face of the country's economic contraction, the unthinkable suddenly makes sense. "Can we develop beyond this point without importing American ideas about the conception of the individual?" Raslan asks. "Probably not." Fascinated by what he calls "the imagined communities of the American West," he believes Malaysians can reinvent themselves in much the way Americans do: by asserting a new identity that works.

Two months before, halfway around the globe in Provence, France, I meet another enthusiast of all things American, Marc Lassus. He is the chief of Gemplus, a manufacturer of "smart cards," which can be used as electronic money to purchase telephone time or to store information such as medical records. It's nearly midnight, and I watch him exhort his factory workers to act

---

"Americanization" is a more apt term than "globalization" for the increasing concentration of U.S.-based multinational companies operating worldwide.

---

more American. The typical French executive treats manual laborers with veiled contempt, but Lassus revels in them, working the factory floor like a politician. He betrays his nationality only when it comes to greeting the female machine operators: He kisses them lustily.

Lassus fights the impulse to be, in his words, "too Frenchie." Incredibly, he often speaks English on the job and encourages his co-workers to do the same. The company's marketing materials are expressly written in American English, by writers imported from California's Silicon Valley. Lassus has hired an American number-cruncher to push the idea that the bottom line matters as much in France as it does in the States. Because the French are famously chauvinistic, I am astonished by Lassus' frank admiration of American ways. His e-mail handle says it all: John Wayne.

Thailand, Malaysia, and France aren't unique in their emulation of the United States. "Americanization" is a more apt term than "globalization" for the increasing concentration of U.S.-based multinational companies operating worldwide. Pundits glibly assert that different societies in the world are becoming more alike as if all were influencing and being influenced in equal measure, creating a kind of global melting pot. I don't see it that way. In the 1990s, the world has Americanized at an unprecedented rate, reaching as far as Borneo.

Of course, Levi's, Nike, and Hollywood have long held international sway. But American influence goes deeper than pop culture. Technology—especially computers, software, and the Internet—is seen as quintessentially American. And the way we do business is now also admired worldwide. Once believed to be in permanent decline, the strongest U.S. companies again dominate global markets. Their stress on profits, efficiency, innovation, and "shareholder value" is the envy of capitalists from Tokyo to Buenos Aires.

The notion of "pay for performance," once rare outside of the U.S., is also catching on. Throughout the world, a growing number of companies are adopting the concept of merit, rewarding employees with a slice of the company's total earnings, given as bonuses rather than wages. Risk-taking and even failure, once cast as pure negatives in Asia and Europe, now are viewed increasingly as preludes to success. Office dress is more casual, corridor talk less formal. The old-boy networks, based on what schools people graduated from (Europe) or which family and personal connections they could draw from (Asia), are slowly breaking down.

For all its seductiveness, however, Americanization has a dark side, an underbelly that perhaps we know better than anyone else.

"Within five to 10 years, these practices won't [just] be American anymore; they will be everywhere," says Roel Pieper, a senior executive at Philips, the Dutch electronics multinational.

American social and political ideas are also taking hold. At a time when Japan—hugely influential in the 1980s—is stagnant, the American willingness to improvise is trumping the virtues of traditionalism. Countries such as Japan and Germany, where the concept of nationality is rooted in the racially based idea of bloodlines, are starting to accept that a polyglot country such as the United States has fundamental advantages.

Scholars throughout Europe now vie to publish their articles in American journals. In Berlin, worried parents recently convinced educators to begin teaching English in the first grade rather than waiting until the third. And in Penang, Malaysia, primary schools stage storytelling competitions—in English.

For all its seductiveness, however, Americanization has a dark side, an underbelly that perhaps we know better than anyone else. And as Americans, who can blame us for asking whether the relentless spread of our values is worth the price?

It is a warm September evening in Washington, D.C., and I am sitting on an outdoor patio at a fashionable restaurant, the Tabard Inn. My companion is Andrea Durbin, director of international programs for Friends of the Earth. She is part of a broad movement that opposed NAFTA (unsuccessfully), helped kill fast-track (Clinton's effort to gain a free hand in negotiating trade pacts), and is now trying to bring the International Monetary Fund to heel. The IMF recently won an $18 billion commitment from Congress to replenish reserves exhausted by the fund's successive bailouts of

Thailand, South Korea, Indonesia, and Russia. An unusual alliance of conservatives and radicals forced the fund, as a condition of this new cash infusion, to provide more information about its inner workings, which may make it easier for critics to track how the IMF protects U.S. investors and promotes an American capitalism.

The IMF generally opposes trade barriers, low interest rates, and deficit spending. These policies, Durbin points out, have led the IMF to mishandle the global capitalist crisis that began with a whimper in July 1997 when the Thai baht collapsed. Using a formula wholeheartedly endorsed by the U.S. Department of the Treasury, the IMF drove Thai interest rates sky-high in a bid to protect the baht, strangling liquidity in a banking system rife with cronyism. At the same time, the fund and the U.S. insisted on new bankruptcy laws-leading to a fire sale of sorts and freeing the way for foreign companies, including American ones, to snap up assets, such as Thai car companies, on the cheap.

The dollarization of the world economy is just one aspect of the Pyrrhic victory of the worldwide spread of American values.

The story is the same elsewhere in the world. The result is that world capitalism is in shambles. In Brazil and Mexico, living standards are falling and stock markets are in disarray even though governments have curtailed spending on social services and privatized essential public monopolies. In Indonesia, a quarter century of rising living standards was reversed during the Asian financial crisis, while an IMF "rescue" program succeeded only in helping to bankrupt the country. In Russia, after the IMF's "help," the ruble collapsed. The dollar is now king; it greases so much commerce that some argue that the greenback should be the official currency. (The dark side of the American global dream is particularly obvious in one former Soviet republic, Moldova.) All over the world, meanwhile, the moneyed classes are converting local currencies into dollars and shipping them to the United States. According to the Federal Reserve Board, about two-thirds of all U.S. currency (the bills themselves) circulate abroad—an estimated $300 billion. The dollarization of the world economy is just one aspect of the Pyrrhic victory of the worldwide spread of American values. Durbin ticks off her own list of the worst aspects of Americanization:

Inequality: The American economic model has led to increasing disparities of wealth and income. Both stock options and pay for performance are becoming popular in Europe, where, in a number of countries, inequality is rising even faster than in the U.S., according to the Luxembourg Income Study, the leading source on the subject. "The U.S. still has the most inequality based on income," says Timothy Smeeding, an economist at Syracuse University. But, incredibly, even Denmark and Sweden have seen income gaps widen more rapidly than in the U.S. That's partly because, as in most other countries, Scandinavians are paying much higher wages to skilled workers and squeezing labor costs at the bottom.

Consumerism: U.S. per capita consumption is up to 20 times greater than in the developing world. "If even half the world's people achieve the American way of life," says Durbin, "we'll have an environmental disaster on our hands." This is a critical point: According to the World Resources Institute, the U.S. consumes a quarter of the world's oil, a third of its paper, and 40 percent of its beef and veal. If such patterns are replicated—say in China alone—the effect on world resources will be dramatic.

Cultural monotony: When a second-tier NBA player like Kobe Bryant merits giant billboards in Paris, the mania for U.S. culture has gone too far. "Our culture is such a strong one it tends to dominate and erode other cultures," Durbin says. "They have a lot to contribute to the international dialogue, but we're losing them."

> *Imitators of the U.S. rightfully worry about the price of American cultural domination.*

Imitators of the U.S. rightfully worry about the price of American cultural domination. Consider Germany. One sunny Saturday morning, I am drinking a café au lait on Munich's main square, watching as a glockenspiel strikes noon and sends a small, mechanical army parading around the old tower, attracting tourists. Just off the square, though, German shoppers are pouring into a Disney store, packed with Pocahontas purses, Mickey Mouse towels, and Winnie-the-Pooh dresses. Germans at least have a sense of irony about iconic American brands. It's more distressing to visit some of the most remote river villages of Borneo, as I did a year ago, and find evidence of a bizarre love affair with Americana.

One steamy afternoon, I take a high-speed riverboat to Marudi, a logging town that serves as the hub for various jungle tribes, many of whose members still live in longhouses and follow traditional customs. Seated across from me is an old Orang Ulu woman. Her body is covered with brightly colored tattoos, and her ears are elongated, the result of attaching heavy weights to her lobes. Once the boat hits its cruising speed, the captain puts a video into the ship's TV. It shows professional wrestlers from the United States. Two big white guys with long hair toss each other around the ring. The Orang Ulu woman howls with laughter, her face brightening each time a big hulk falls to the canvas. Hers is no isolated affection. I spend that evening with a militant anti-logging activist in Marudi—a Kayan tribe member considered so dangerous by the government that it had seized his passport. After dinner, he invites me into his house and, with geckos running up and down his walls, plays a traditional Kayan guitar for me. When I tell him about the woman, he confesses that he, too, loves watching American wrestling. So does everyone in the longhouses.

Environmentalists enjoy painting these native people as idyllic traditionalists, but the truth is that they want a piece of America too—but on their own terms. Their resistance to resource exploitation is certainly authentic, and their logging blockades deserve the wholehearted support of outsiders. Yet for these tribespeople, the biggest symbol of progress is American-made: the Johnson outboard motor. Once these river tribes used long poles to push their boats up the region's shallow rivers. How much happier many of them are now with a craft powered by a small motor. Far from looking bucolic, they resemble edgy Long Islanders, speeding back and forth on the water, their ungainly poles snugly on the bottom of their thin, low boats.

Americanization seems unstoppable. Resistance is rising, however. The governments of France and Germany are taking steps to address the inequities fostered by their own embrace of the American model. Both are raising taxes on wealthy people and corporations and, in France's case, paying people the same amount for working fewer hours. In September, Malaysia, long a haven for U.S. investment, slapped controls on its currency, making it harder on foreign investors. Even cultural rebellions are taking place: The Israeli government announced in November that it may require its radio stations to devote half their airtime to songs sung in Hebrew in order to slow down Israel's cultural shift toward Americanization.

> *"Sometimes I feel you're exporting the worst of America."*— Simon Tay, a member of Singapore's parliament.

The pervasiveness of Americanization, in other words, doesn't mean the world will end up full of Clint Eastwoods. Many foreigners drawn to U.S. values and practices are nonetheless disturbed that the U.S. often exports its pathologies. Consider the attitude of Simon Tay, a lawyer and member of parliament in Singapore. In a country where Western values are relentlessly criticized, Tay's admiration for American society stands out. He has a degree from Harvard University and has published a book about his travels in the United States. Yet as we sip cold drinks on a patio outside a mammoth high-rise this spring, he tells me, "Sometimes I feel you're exporting the worst of America."

He mentions the traits that many people in Singapore equate with the American Way: violence, workaholism, disrespect for authority, an endless obsession with instant gratification. Tay realizes that this image of the U.S., gleaned from American movies and television, is something of a caricature. "In your movies and your materialism, we don't see the real America," he admits.

Like many in Asia, he hungers for a more freewheeling society, one that can respect tradition while breaking free from it when necessary. He fears that the so-called Asian miracle came undone partly because rigid Asian societies can hamper American-style creativity. In Singapore, however, the drive to acquire the more eccentric aspects of American life borders on parody. Many years ago, the government banned street performers, considering them beggars. When Tay returned from his stay in the U.S., the sterility of Singapore's streets—all orderly and clean, with no one present without a purpose—weighed on him. In 1997 the government permitted street performers for the first time, but then the government drew a line, requiring performers to audition before a national board. Not only that, whatever money they collected had to be donated to charity. "This is crazy," says Tay. "It's a good example of the tension between wanting a livelier Singapore and maintaining control." (Later, following criticism from Tay and others, the government relaxed the conditions.)

Clearly, says Tay, foreigners may imitate Americans, but that doesn't mean they automatically become like them. This, he concludes, may help preserve Singapore's own cultural traditions as it integrates American ones. "If American values aren't imposed on us, but come in a softer way, I'd welcome that," he says.

But that isn't likely. The global capitalist crisis paradoxically reinforces the power of the United States. Foreign assets are cheaper than they've been in decades. Before the crisis runs its course—and it may take years—U.S. investors may own a much bigger chunk of the developing world: from factories to mines to forests to auto loans, all picked up for a song.

As the century comes to an end, U.S. power stands at a new pinnacle, only this time victory isn't measured in the defeat of an ideological foe but in the influence gained over the world's wealth, culture, and individual identity. If the bulk of the 20th century was defined by military might, its last decade may be summed up by this maxim: "We are all Americans now, like it or not."

A World Together[3]

By Erla Zwingle
National Geographic, August 1999

Once I started looking for them, these moments were every-where: That I should be sitting in a coffee shop in London drinking Italian espresso served by an Algerian waiter to the strains of the Beach Boys singing "I wish they all could be California girls. . . ." Or hanging around a pub in New Delhi that serves Lebanese cui-sine to the music of a Filipino band in rooms decorated with bar-rels of Irish stout, a stuffed hippo head, and a vintage poster announcing the Grand Ole Opry concert to be given at the high school in Douglas, Georgia. Some Japanese are fanatics for fla-menco. Denmark imports five times as much Italian pasta as it did ten years ago. The classic American blond Barbie doll now comes in some 30 national varieties—and this year emerged as Austrian and Moroccan.

Today we are in the throes of a worldwide reformation of cul-tures, a tectonic shift of habits and dreams called, in the curious argot of social scientists, "globalization." It's an inexact term for a wild assortment of changes in politics, business, health, entertain-ment. "Modern industry has established the world market. . . . All old-established national industries . . . are dislodged by new indus-tries whose . . . products are consumed, not only at home, but in every quarter of the globe. In place of the old wants . . . we find new wants, requiring for their satisfaction the products of distant lands and climes." Karl Marx and Friedrich Engels wrote this 150 years ago in *The Communist Manifesto.* Their statement now describes an ordinary fact of life.

How people feel about this depends a great deal on where they live and how much money they have. Yet globalization, as one report stated, "is a reality, not a choice." Humans have been weav-ing commercial and cultural connections since before the first camel caravan ventured afield. In the 19th century the postal ser-vice, newspapers, transcontinental railroads, and great steam-powered ships wrought fundamental changes. Telegraph, telephone, radio, and television tied tighter and more intricate

---

knots between individuals and the wider world. Now computers, the Internet, cellular phones, cable TV, and cheaper jet transportation have accelerated and complicated these connections.

Still, the basic dynamic remains the same: Goods move. People move. Ideas move. And cultures change. The difference now is the speed and scope of these changes. It took television 13 years to acquire 50 million users; the Internet took only five.

Not everyone is happy about this. Some Western social scientists and anthropologists, and not a few foreign politicians, believe that a sort of cultural cloning will result from what they regard as the "cultural assault" of McDonald's, Coca-Cola, Disney, Nike, MTV, and the English language itself—more than a fifth of all the people in the world now speak English to some degree. Whatever their backgrounds or agendas, these critics are convinced that Western—often equated with American—influences will flatten every cultural crease, producing, as one observer terms it, one big "McWorld."

> *Westernization ... is a phenomenon shot through with inconsistencies and populated by very strange bedfellows.*

Popular factions sprout to exploit nationalist anxieties. In China, where xenophobia and economic ambition have often struggled for the upper hand, a recent book called *China Can Say No* became a best-seller by attacking what it considers the Chinese willingness to believe blindly in foreign things, advising Chinese travelers to not fly on a Boeing 777 and suggesting that Hollywood be burned.

There are many Westerners among the denouncers of Western cultural influences, but James Watson, a Harvard anthropologist, isn't one of them. "The lives of Chinese villagers I know are infinitely better now than they were 30 years ago," he says. "China has become more open partly because of the demands of ordinary people. They want to become part of the world—I would say globalism is the major force for democracy in China. People want refrigerators, stereos, CD players. I feel it's a moral obligation not to say: 'Those people out there should continue to live in a museum while we will have showers that work.'"

Westernization, I discovered over months of study and travel, is a phenomenon shot through with inconsistencies and populated by very strange bedfellows. Critics of Western culture blast Coke and Hollywood but not organ transplants and computers. Boosters of Western culture can point to increased efforts to preserve and protect the environment. Yet they make no mention of some less salubrious aspects of Western culture, such as cigarettes and automobiles, which, even as they are being eagerly adopted in the developing world, are having disastrous effects. Apparently westernization is not a straight road to hell, or to paradise either.

But I also discovered that cultures are as resourceful, resilient, and unpredictable as the people who compose them. In Los Angeles, the ostensible fountainhead of world cultural degradation, I saw more diversity than I could ever have supposed—at Hollywood High School the student body represents 32 different languages. In Shanghai I found that the television show Sesame Street has been redesigned by Chinese educators to teach Chinese values and traditions. "We borrowed an American box," one told me, "and put Chinese content into it." In India, where there are more than 400 languages and several very strict religions, McDonald's serves mutton instead of beef and offers a vegetarian menu acceptable to even the most orthodox Hindu.

"I used to say that Peoria will look like Paris, and Beijing will look like Boston," said Marshall W. Fishwick, professor of American studies at Virginia Tech, "but now I'm not so sure."

> *Incorrigibly curious, ravenous for novelty, Americans love to experiment with ethnic food, clothes, words.*

For hundreds of years, women in Africa, the Middle East, and South Asia have decorated their bodies with designs painted with a paste made from henna leaves. In India this practice is called "mehndi." It's also called mehndi in Los Angeles, and as I write, it is considered a very cool thing to do, though by the time you read this it may have followed the love song from Titanic into oblivion.

One sunny September afternoon I was sitting in a spacious frame house in West Hollywood watching a French artist named Pascal Giacomini carefully draw swirls down the bare arm of a Hispanic girl to the rhythm of Brazilian samba music. "It's a temporary, painless tattoo—in two weeks it's gone," Pascal explained softly as he concentrated on the little dots he was making around the curving tendrils near her elbow. "Henna is tied to a wedding tradition, and it has no connection with drugs or rock-and-roll. It's an art form with roots. Now it's hugely popular—in Japan, Argentina, Sweden, Greece. My Guatemalan maid does it. . . ."

He took my left hand and drew a sinuous uncoiling circle; it trailed down my middle finger and ended with a dot at the cuticle.

Pascal has developed a mehndi kit, which he sells through Learningsmith and more than a hundred other outlets. "In America, people will grab anything and run with it," Pascal said. Incorrigibly curious, ravenous for novelty, Americans love to experiment with ethnic food, clothes, words. Mehndi is just one of the many bits of exotica to become the mall rat's latest diversion. And when something becomes fashion, it becomes commercial.

The critical mass of teenagers—800 million in the world, the most there have ever been—with time and money to spend is one of the powerful engines of merging global cultures. Kids travel, they hang out, and above all they buy stuff. I'm sorry to say I failed to discover who was the first teenager to put his baseball cap on backward. Or the first one to copy him. But I do know that rap music, which sprang from the inner-city ghettos, began making big money only when rebellious white teenagers started buying it. But how can anyone predict what kids are going to want? Companies urgently need to know, so consultants have sprung up to forecast trends. They're called "cool hunters," and Amanda Freeman took me in hand one morning to explain how it works.

> *"Fusion is going to be the huge term that everybody's going to use."*— **Amanda Freeman of Youth Intelligence.**

Amanda, who is 22, works for a New York-based company called Youth Intelligence and has come to Los Angeles to conduct one of three annual surveys, whose results go to such clients as Sprint and MTV. She has shoulder-length brown hair and is wearing a knee-length brocade skirt and simple black wrap top. Amanda looks very cool to me, but she says no. "The funny thing about my work is that you don't have to be cool to do it," she says. "You just have to have the eye."

We go to a smallish '50s-style diner in Los Feliz, a slightly seedy pocket east of Hollywood that has just become trendy. Then we wander through a few of the thrift shops. "If it's not going to be affordable," Amanda remarks, "it's never going to catch on."

What trends does she see forming now? "People aren't as health conscious as they were, so we're seeing fondue and crepes," she answers. "Another trend—the home is becoming more of a social place again. And travel's huge right now—you go to a place and bring stuff back.

"It's really hard to be original these days, so the easiest way to come up with new stuff is to mix things that already exist. Fusion is going to be the huge term that everybody's going to use," she concludes. "There's going to be more blending, like Spanish music and punk—things that are so unrelated."

Los Angeles is fusion central, where cultures mix and morph. Take Tom Sloper and mah-jongg. Tom is a computer geek who is also a mah-jongg fanatic. This being America, he has found a way to marry these two passions and sell the result. He has designed a software program, Shanghai: Dynasty, that enables you to play mah-jongg on the Internet. This ancient Chinese game involves both strategy and luck, and it is still played all over Asia in small rooms that are full of smoke and the ceaseless click of the chunky plastic tiles and the fierce concentration of the players. It is also played by rich society women at country clubs in Beverly Hills and in apartments on Manhattan's Upper West Side. But Tom, 50, was playing it at his desk in Los Angeles one evening in the silence of a nearly empty office building.

Actually, he only appeared to be alone. His glowing computer screen showed a game already in progress with several habitual partners: "Blue Whale," a man in Cologne, Germany, where the local time was 4:30 a.m.; Russ, from Dayton, Ohio; and "yobydderf" (or Freddyboy spelled backward), a Chinese-American who lives in Edina, Minnesota. (According to one study 64 percent of Asian-American families are linked to the Internet, compared with 33 percent of all U.S. families.) Tom played effortlessly as we talked.

"I've learned about 11 different styles of mah-jongg," he told me with that detached friendliness of those whose true connection is with machines. "There are a couple of different ways of playing it in America. We usually play Chinese mah-jongg. The Japanese style is the most challenging—more hoops to jump through."

I watched the little tiles, like the cards in solitaire, bounce around the screen. From what I gathered, it has to do with collecting similar or sequential tiles of dots, characters, bamboos, winds, or dragons into groupings called pungs, kongs, or, in some cases, chows. As Tom played, he and his partners conversed by typing short comments to each other.

"I'm trying to coax Fred to be a better sport—he kind of gloats too much when he wins, and he really likes the Spice Girls too," Tom remarked as his fingers gripped the mouse. "Oh, he got a pung of dragons, I hate him. . . ." The mouse clicked, some tiles shifted.

Does he ever play with real people? "Oh yeah," Tom replied. "Once a week at the office in the evening, and Thursday at lunch." A new name appeared on the screen. "There's Fred's mother. Can't be, they're in Vegas. Oh, it must be his sister. There's my eight dot. TJ's online too, she's the one from Wales—a real night owl. She's getting married soon, and she lives with her fiance, and sometimes he gets up and says, 'Get off that damn computer!'"

Tom played on into the night. At least it was night where I was. He, an American playing a Chinese game with people in Germany, Wales, Ohio, and Minnesota, was up in the cybersphere far above the level of time zones. It is a realm populated by individuals he's never met who may be more real to him than the people who live next door. "Can't be, they're in Vegas." The global village gets a fiber-optic party line.

If it seems that life in the West has become a fast-forward blur, consider China. In just 20 years, since market forces were unleashed by economic reforms begun in 1978, life for many urban Chinese has changed drastically. A recent survey of 12 major cities showed that 97 percent of the respondents had televisions, and 88 percent had refrigerators and washing machines. Another study revealed that farmers are eating 48 percent more meat each year and 400 percent more fruit. Cosmopolitan magazine, plunging necklines and all, is read by 260,000 Chinese women every month.

I went to Shanghai to see how the cultural trends show up in the largest city in the world's most populous nation. It is also a city that has long been open to the West. General Motors, for example, set up its first Buick sales outlet in Shanghai in 1929; today GM has invested 1.5 billion dollars in a new plant there, the biggest Sino-American venture in China.

Once a city of elegant villas and imposing beaux arts office buildings facing the river with shoulders squared, Shanghai is currently ripping itself to ribbons. In a decade scores of gleaming new skyscrapers have shot up to crowd and jostle the skyline, cramp the narrow winding streets, and choke the parks and open spaces with their sheer soaring presence (most are 80 percent vacant). Traffic crawls, even on the new multilane overpasses. But on the streets the women are dressed in bright colors, and many carry several shopping bags, especially on the Nanjing Road, which is lined with boutiques and malls. In its first two weeks of business the Gucci store took in a surprising $100,000.

"Maybe young women today don't know what it was like," says Wu Ying, editor in chief of the Chinese edition of the French fashion magazine Elle. "But ten years ago I wouldn't have imagined myself wearing this blouse." It was red, with white polka dots. "When people bought clothes, they thought 'How long will it last?' A housewife knew that most of the monthly salary would be spent on food, and now it's just a small part, so she can think about what to wear or where to travel. And now with refrigerators, we don't have to buy food every day."

As for the cultural dislocation this might bring: "People in Shanghai don't see it as a problem," said a young German businessman. "The Chinese are very good at dealing with ambiguity. It's accepted—'It's very different, but it's OK, so, so what?'"

Li Ping is a cardiologist who discovered Amway cosmetics two years ago and began what Americans call selling door-to-door. Because it's very difficult for an individual to start a business, direct sales have become the new road to prosperity for many enterprising Chinese. As incomes and curiosity about Western products have grown, companies such as Amway, Avon, Tupperware, and Mary

Kay have made swift inroads. Amway, for example, has some 92,000 sales representatives who made almost one hundred million dollars in sales in 1998.

I went with Dr. Li to visit some of her clients. A compact, robust, middle-aged woman wearing a stylish white cotton dress with little brass stars scattered over the shoulders, Dr. Li made no secret of her enthusiasm for her new avocation. "In the past every person had a dream that they could do what they want," she said, "but they couldn't, because tradition wouldn't allow them to do it. I hope to build a clinic for myself in the future. So I have to earn extra money, and Amway is a good chance. Because money doesn't fall from heaven."

Mrs. Gong Suihua has been a client for a year. She lives with her husband in a comfortable apartment with polished wood floors and two bedrooms; there is also a large Panasonic television with Sony speakers. She offered us coffee and pulled out photographs of her daughter in Los Angeles. Then Mrs. Gong settled down for a demonstration of the new facial products—cleanser and cream. "Age will destroy our skin. We need to take care of it," Dr. Li says as she works on her friend's face. "I'm a doctor, so I have some knowledge about beauty."

Mrs. Gong didn't take long to order several items. "I know the quality is very great," she said. "Even if the price is high, it's worth it. We feel confident buying this way because friends introduce the products."

The morning passed quickly. It seemed so unremarkable that I had to remind myself how revolutionary it really was. "This way has put new ideas into people's brains," Dr. Li said, her eyes shining. "It is helping you tap all your potential."

Potential: This is largely a Western concept. Set aside the makeup and skyscrapers, and it's clear that the truly great leap forward here is at the level of ideas. To really grasp this, I had only to witness the local performance of Shakespeare's Macbeth by the Hiu Kok Drama Association from Macau. There we were at the Shanghai Theatre Academy, some 30 professors and students of literature and drama from all over China and I, on folding chairs around a space not unlike half of a basketball court. "I'm not going to be much help," murmured Zhang Fang, my interpreter. "I don't understand the Cantonese language, and most of these people don't either."

I had spoken earlier with the young director, Hui Koc Kun, known as Billy. He chose Macbeth, he said, because it represents so perfectly the current situation in Macau. This year the Portuguese colony will become part of China, and this is generating a great deal of anxiety. "I wanted to show the feeling of contradiction," he explained in tentative English. "Macbeth is a general. He's a hero. He wants to do the right thing. But everything takes him to a road—he doesn't want to be on that road, but things want him to take that path. The war, the environment, his wife. We have no choice in the modern city. You think you can choose, but actually you have no choice."

I thought I knew what to watch for, but the only characters I recognized were the three witches. Otherwise the small group, dressed in leotards and capes, spent most of an hour running in circles, leaping, and threatening to beat each other with long sticks. The lighting was heavy on shadows, with frequent strobelike flashes. Language wasn't a problem, as the actors mainly snarled and shrieked. Then they turned their backs to the audience and a few shouted "Free Macau!" in Cantonese. The lights went out, and for a moment the only sound in the darkness was the whirring of an expensive camera on auto-rewind.

This is China? It could have been a college campus anywhere in the West: the anguished students, the dubious adults, the political exploitation of the massacred classic. Until recently such a performance was unthinkable. It strained imagination that this could be the same country where a generation ago the three most desired luxury items were wristwatches, bicycles, and sewing machines.

Early on I realized that I was going to need some type of compass to guide me through the wilds of global culture. So when I was in Los Angeles, I sought out Alvin Toffler, whose book *Future Shock* was published in 1970. In the nearly three decades since, he has developed and refined a number of interesting ideas, explained in *The Third Wave*, written with his wife, Heidi.

What do we know about the future now, I asked, that we didn't know before? "We now know that order grows out of chaos," he answered immediately. "You cannot have significant change, especially on the scale of Russia or China, without conflict. Not conflicts between East and West, or North and South, but 'wave' conflicts between industrially dominant countries and predominantly agrarian countries, or conflicts within countries making a transition from one to the other."

Waves, he explained, are major changes in civilization. The first wave came with the development of agriculture, the second with industry. Today we are in the midst of the third, which is based on information. "In 1956 something new began to happen, which amounts to the emergence of a new civilization," Toffler said. It was in that year that U.S. service and knowledge workers outnumbered blue-collar factory workers. In 1957 Sputnik went up. Then jet aviation became commercial, television became universal, and computers began to be widely used. And with all these changes came changes in culture.

"What's happening now is the trisection of world power," he continued. "Agrarian nations on the bottom, smokestack countries in between, and knowledge-based economies on top." There are a number of countries—Brazil, for example—where all three civilizations coexist and collide.

"Culturally we'll see big changes," Toffler said. "You're going to turn on your TV and get Nigerian TV and Fijian TV in your own language." Also, some experts predict that the TV of the future, with 500 cable channels, may be used by smaller groups to foster their separate, distinctive cultures and languages.

"People ask, 'Can we become third wave and still remain Chinese?' Yes," Toffler says. "You can have a unique culture made of your core culture. But you'll be the Chinese of the future, not of the past."

While some politicians rail against "cultural pollution," they make no mention of the fact that many foreign companies have "gone native."

Rajan Bakshi is a good example of the Indian of the future. He is a lawyer and a cable TV entrepreneur in New Delhi, brash, energetic, and making money. He, for one, has no interest in clinging to India's vast and elaborate past. "I think periodic upheavals are part of the regeneration process," he told me. "No culture exists in a vacuum. It all comes from somewhere. Ancient customs were modern at one time."

India, like China, teems with a billion people. But the contrast between the traditional and the new seems sharper and more ironic in a country that has nuclear power but no four-lane highways linking its major cities; that has some four million doctors and ranks among the world's top five countries in computer software production but where nearly half the population can't read or write.

In 1991 India began opening its economy to wider trade, and the United States quickly became its primary trading and investment partner—687 million dollars invested in 1997, almost three times as much as the year before. But promoters of global culture may have expected too much. Foreign companies were thrilled by sheer numbers—an estimated 150 million potential middle-income consumers—without knowing that "middle income" in India often connotes an annual per capita amount of only about 1,500 dollars. Many multinationals, from McDonald's to Panasonic, have had to accept paper-thin profit margins to stay afloat in India.

And while some politicians rail against "cultural pollution," they make no mention of the fact that many foreign companies have "gone native." Revlon, for instance, has adapted the color palette and composition of its cosmetics to suit the Indian skin and climate, and when MTV added an India-dedicated network with Indian performers, its ratings jumped. In Rajan Bakshi's opinion, foreign companies have also brought better job opportunities: "I think the average worker is better off with the multinationals," he said. "I see these young people at the satellite companies—girls who are 24, 25. If they'd been working for an Indian company, they'd have been exploited. Smart young people now have options because of the multinationals."

> *"We don't care about multinationals. I can't feed my children."*—
> Kahida Khatoon, a resident of Jamnuna Basti, India.

Anyway, Bakshi isn't impressed by the interminable debates about cultural purity. Neither is Yogendra Singh, a retired sociology professor, who explained: "India has lived with cultural pluralism for centuries. In fact, the history of India is based on linkages with other cultures."

Early one hot October morning I made my way along the banks of New Delhi's Yamuna River to Jamuna Basti, a massive slum that swarms with hundreds of thousands of destitute people, many of them migrants from Bangladesh and the state of Bihar. The preoccupations of politicians and intellectuals—whether the government should block international calls that offer phone sex, say, or whether English is making India's national languages "look inadequate"—had yet to reach this outpost. Everyone here was talking about the astronomical price of onions. Almost overnight the cost reportedly spiked tenfold, and without onions you can hardly make anything worth eating.

Santosh Kumar, a 16-year-old boy who earns a hundred rupees ($2.34) a day driving a bicycle ricksha, led me to the riverbanks where the "dhobis," or washermen, were working. The Yamuna was beige, loaded with detritus and raw sewage. Along the shore men and women were laboring over wet piles of clothes. Each dhobi took a heavy handful of laundry, hauled it out of the water, and swung it through the air, slinging it down hard against a block of reddish stone.

Walking on, we passed a cafe where a boy was stirring tea in a large pot. The cafe wasn't big, but at least it had two rooms. The hundreds of dwellings clustered around it were no more than rectangular patches of concrete with three low walls made of cinder block or brick or matting. Many were missing the front wall, so I could see straight into the back.

From the cafe came the unexpected glow of a black-and-white TV. Rajnai, the burly owner, was lounging in the doorway. He said he'd gotten the TV "to indulge his son."

"I paid 500 rupees for it secondhand," he said. "We watch mostly films and news." I looked surprised. "It's no big deal," he shrugged. "A lot of houses have television."

As we talked, a crowd quickly formed around me, and a slender, gray-haired woman named Zahida Khatoon pushed to the front. I asked what she thought of Coke and Pepsi. "If those companies come in and the local people benefit," she answered, "I don't object. But while the government is levying huge taxes on these foreign goods, we can't afford to send our kids to school. We don't care about multinationals. I can't feed my children. Our 'cultural roots'—it doesn't concern me."

I got into the car and headed back toward the main road, moving slowly through the masses of people, the cows, the dogs, the toddlers. A group of teenage boys squeezed past. One of them was wearing a T-shirt emblazoned "Titanic." I had to know why. He grinned shyly.

Linking: This is what the spread of global culture ultimately means.

Had he seen the movie? "No," he replied. Did he know the story? "Not really," he said. "But my friend told me about it."

But why, I wondered, would a boy want to wear a T-shirt advertising something he knew nothing about, that represented no experience he'd ever had, that referred to nothing that mattered to him? The shirt, it occurred to me, didn't link him to the movie (or that damn song) or even to the West at large. But it did link him to his friend.

Linking: This is what the spread of global culture ultimately means. Goods will continue to move—from 1987 to 1995 local economies in California exported 200 percent more products, businesses in Idaho 375 percent more. People move: It is cheaper for businesses to import talented employees than to train people at home. Ideas move: In Japan a generation of children raised with interactive computer games has sensed, at least at the cyber level, new possibilities. "What this exposure has given them is a direct sense . . . of asking the 'what if' questions they could never comfortably ask before (because of the Shinto superstition that saying a thing would make it happen)," wrote Kenichi Ohmae in *The End of the Nation State.* "The implicit message in all this . . . is that it is possible to actively take control of one's situation or circumstances and, thereby, to change one's fate. . . . For the Japanese, this is an entirely new way of thinking."

Change: It's a reality, not a choice. But what will be its true driving force? Cultures don't become more uniform; instead, both old and new tend to transform each other. The late philosopher Isaiah Berlin believed that, rather than aspire to some utopian ideal, a society should strive for something else: "not that we agree with each other," his biographer explained, "but that we can understand each other."

In Shanghai one October evening I joined a group gathered in a small, sterile hotel meeting room. It was the eve of Yom Kippur, the Jewish Day of Atonement, and there were diplomats, teachers, and businessmen from many Western countries. Elegant women with lively children, single men, young fathers. Shalom Greenberg, a young Jew from Israel married to an American, was presiding over his first High Holy Days as rabbi of the infant congregation.

"It's part of the Jewish history that Jews went all over the world," Rabbi Greenberg reflected. "They received a lot from local cultures, but they also kept their own identity."

The solemn liturgy proceeded, unchanged over thousands of years and hundreds of alien cultures: "Create in me a clean heart, O God, and renew a right spirit within me," he intoned. I'm neither Jewish nor Chinese, but sitting there I didn't feel foreign—I felt at home. The penitence may have been Jewish, but the aspiration was universal.

Global culture doesn't mean just more TV sets and Nike shoes. Linking is humanity's natural impulse, its common destiny. But the ties that bind people around the world are not merely technological or commercial. They are the powerful cords of the heart.

Global Culture[4]

Forget the Asian-Western Distinction. We Think Alike.

FAR EASTERN ECONOMIC REVIEW, JULY 22, 1999

Following China's Belgrade embassy bombing, foreign newspapers quickly noted that even as Chinese students were hurling rocks at America's own legation in Beijing, their countrymen were happily wolfing down hamburgers and French fries at McDonald's. Such was the contradiction of the Chinese's love-hate relationship with America. Only not. While a newly arrived American in Asia, for example, may see in the familiar fast-food outlet a bit of America on foreign soil, many Asians wouldn't. Practically all the original American outlets are adapting to the Asian palate, begging the question of how "American" they are. Pizza Hut offers curried meat, spicy shrimp and corn toppings in several Asian countries. In Hong Kong, it lets you substitute Thousand-Island dressing for the traditional tomato-sauce base. Besides the staple of Big Macs, McDonald's serves up local variants of fast food. In Malaysia, where chicken is the one meat item that may be consumed by all ethnic and religious groups in the country, you can order fried chicken. As for the ultimate fried-chicken outlet, it has even dropped "Kentucky" from its name, opting for the colourless "KFC." In short, there is little that's really "American" about these outlets. More, Burger King is now British-owned; the successful Jollibee chain is homegrown in the Philippines. What all this indicates is not that "American" fast-food outlets have been clever at marketing. (They are, but that's a separate issue.) More significant is what they tell us about the way our global culture has evolved at the popular level.

Only those who still insist on an imperialist-inspired conspiracy to take over the world would see in these fast-food outlets, blue jeans, Coca-Cola and other facets of pop culture, the evil multinationals' attempt to hook Asians on foreign products. To their countrymen, a Big Mac or Whopper today is about as exotic as fried rice. And then again no one complains about the pervasiveness of Western dress, particularly the adoption of the T-shirt as a global

---

4. Article from *Far Eastern Economic Review,* July 22, 1999. Copyright © *Far Eastern Economic Review.* Reprinted with permission.

uniform. (As for the latter, no good anti-imperialist would be without one emblazoned with the scowling image of Che Guevara.) More, does anyone seriously identify the electric light bulb with Thomas Edison's America? And listen to pop music from Thailand, Indonesia, Hong Kong, Taiwan and Japan. There is little that's Asian about it except for the language it is sung in. The fact is that what we today consider "local" or "foreign" is a matter of choice. Unfortunately, this choice of perception gets in the way of considering how remarkably connected Asia is with the rest of the globe.

Today, there is little in our world that is culturally unalloyed and wholly indigenous. But while globalization is more accepted at the pop-culture level, it is less acknowledged elsewhere. For one, it is remarkable how uniformly the world thinks. Modern Asia is built upon the foundation of originally Western-derived concepts. For example, though Asian science recognized cause-and-effect relations in natural phenomena, historians continue to dicker over why it didn't go one step further and derive laws and hypotheses that could be used to control and better use nature. Whatever the reason, it's no wonder then that much of traditional Asian architecture, for example, seems so much in harmony with nature. But modern Asian buildings airily defy gravity in a way only possible if one were to design and build with full conviction in how Newton's mechanics works. To reach this state involves thinking less in an indigenous manner.

Just like pop culture, Asian conceptual thinking involving mathematics has absorbed and internalized what some would call "Western" methods. Indeed, Asia's industrialization and economic expansion is predicated on people in our region internalizing the mathematical and scientific norms that first emerged in the West. That Asia itself now has contributed to advances here shows how we have become a part of this scientific culture.

Thus it may be time to stop thinking of Asian vs. Western. To be sure, Asia isn't about to look like Europe or America—in the same way that London and New York have their individual character. But in significant areas, the distinction between East and West is marginal. It's on the scale of the difference between wonton noodle soup and a quarter pounder with fries to an Asian diner. Not much difference at all. Welcome to the new world.

V. What's Up, Doc?
Global Science

Editor's Introduction

No book on globalization would be complete without a section on science. The wonders and discoveries in the high-technology field are hinted at in Section II, as businesses scramble to keep up with the demands of instant communication and global access to the Internet. This section centers on the effects of globalization on health care and the environment. Nearly instantaneous communication has revolutionized medicine. Researchers and doctors can share information more easily now, and patients even in hard-to-reach areas are being taught about disease prevention and cures. D. Ted Lewers's article "AMA Becomes an International Force in Medicine," reprinted from the *American Medical News*, celebrates America's place in helping to spread new advances in medicine and applauds its position as the standard-bearer for good medical practices. He also congratulates the American Medical Association's role in promoting America's high esteem in this field.

While health care has seen improvements (and some corresponding setbacks), the environment has had its own hurdles to jump. Large manufacturing companies that fled to underdeveloped nations in order to cut operational and labor costs are frequently left to regulate their own ethical standards. This practice of laissez-faire often has a deleterious effect on the environment. The health of the planet is dependent on a healthy environment. Everyone on earth, in all countries, shares the same atmosphere; the denuding of forests in one country will affect the ozone layer of the whole world. In "Seeds of Chaos" (from *Amicus Journal*), Jeff Gersh reviews the state of the environment in a world trying to globalize at the speed of light. While Gersh finds that Western nations have recently begun to show concern for halting the rapid deterioration of the planet's natural resources, he writes that developing countries, in an understandable wish to catch up to their globalized neighbors, commit the mistakes of the Western nations. He reviews the many ways in which globalization harms the environment (including the effects of transporting goods) and explains why people allow poor environmental practices to continue. He concludes with the hope that companies will soon take environmental causes to heart and expresses the belief that underdeveloped countries, once they have caught up, will share the concerns of their globalized counterparts.

The increase in the number of factories, which has contributed to the depletion of natural resources, has had an equally negative effect on plants and animals. Many species alive today could become extinct by the time this book is printed. Jennifer Scarlott writes in "Killing Them Softly," an essay for *E: The*

Environmental Magazine, about the likely extinction of the tiger—just one of the many animals and vegetation endangered by the globalization of the manufacturing industry.

AMA Becomes an International Force in Medicine[1]

BY D. TED LEWERS, MD
AMERICAN MEDICAL NEWS, APRIL 3, 2000

Since joining the AMA Board of Trustees in 1993, I have had the privilege of meeting literally thousands of physicians in every setting imaginable.

In virtually every state in the union, I have talked with physicians in multispecialty group practice, solo practice and every practice configuration in between.

And almost without exception, I find dedicated, hard-working professionals literally consumed by the myriad demands and details of the day-to-day practice of medicine. There are precious few opportunities to look beyond local demands, to take the long view of the art and science of medicine.

But there is a longer view, a global perspective that, in the future, I believe will shape our professional lives more and more.

In his best-selling book, *The Lexus and the Olive Tree, New York Times* foreign affairs columnist Thomas Friedman rightly points out that ours is a new era of globalization, an era that is just 10 years old, dating from the fall of the Berlin Wall.

But for us in the AMA, globalization began decades ago. If anything, globalization is now taking on added significance as traditional national boundaries, traditional ideas, traditional ways of doing our jobs no longer exist and new forms of action and interaction come into play.

The art and science of medicine truly is an international entity. And the AMA truly is an international force. Some examples come easily to hand:

> The *Journal of the American Medical Association* (JAMA) distributes virtually half its editions outside the United States; English is just one of a dozen languages JAMA uses in its 17 editions.

> English is the "lingua franca" of medicine, and American medical information is the world's premier resource, as American medical research, treatment, education and ethics set the standards.

---

1.   Article by D. Ted Lewers, MD, *American Medical News,* April 3, 2000. Copyright © *American Medical News.* Reprinted with permission.

Non-U.S. practitioners recognize the quality of American medicine by sending both their medical students and their patients to the United States.

The number of non-U.S. visits to the AMA Internet site is a large and growing percentage of 1.5 million hits per week.

Members of the World Medical Assn. look first at the AMA's ways of doing things before setting policy, tapping the AMA's experience, policy base and solid research.

Individual governments and medical groups study the AMA to determine how best to re-create local AMAs.

In that spirit, two current examples of AMA globalization underscore the round-the-world reach of what we do.

For us in the AMA, globalization began decades ago.

In August, the AMA will co-sponsor the 11th annual World Conference on Tobacco or Health, recognizing the AMA's worldwide leadership in cutting tobacco consumption.

And the AMA House of Delegates has voted to establish an international membership category. International memberships will foster continuing medical education, the exchange of knowledge and the setting of professional standards worldwide.

The AMA has hosted a number of foreign delegations wanting to know how best to emulate AMA processes. The U.S. State Dept.'s Agency for International Development included AMA representatives in a group sent to help Russian physicians establish certification processes.

Last year, for the first time, AMA advisers were included in the U.S. delegation to the World Health Organization. And each month brings new invitations for the AMA to participate in conferences, symposia, media briefings and other meetings outside the United States.

All of this adds up to a large and growing global presence for the medical profession's leading force.

Management consultant Peter Drucker observed that soon, "there will be two types of CEOs: those who think globally and those who are unemployed."

I won't make a similar prediction for physicians, not only because it would be absurd but also because ours is already a globally thinking—and acting—profession.

Seeds of Chaos[2]

BY JEFF GERSH
AMICUS JOURNAL, SUMMER 1999

In the winter of 1990, I spent a day and a half traveling by bus and truck from Bangkok, and another day hiking up corkscrew footpaths to reach a small Red Karen village in the northwestern hills of Thailand. Tucked into a high perch overlooking rice paddies, eight huts of reed, bamboo, and wood, elevated on stilts, were open to neighbors and friends who wished to visit. One dwelling, however, was padlocked, an odd sight in this remote place. Through its window I could see that the hut was bare—no hammock, no rice sacks or fertilizer. In one corner, as if arranged by some gifted art director to catch the light, sat a wooden soda case holding a few bottles of Coca-Cola.

This was my personal freeze-frame glimpse of globalization in progress. Those Coke bottles, icons of international marketing, represented an early wave of the sea of foreign products and capital that has since washed over Thailand and other developing countries. At the time, Thailand's share of the billions of dollars spent annually on advertising was going through an enormous expansion, growing 300 percent from 1986 to 1996. Recently, Thai consumers have delighted Heinz executives by increasing their yearly spending on ketchup to nearly a dollar per person, almost half the U.S. total. Today, not only is Thailand a sought-after international market, but it is also playing the export game itself, on a grand scale: the nation is now the world's second-largest producer of pickup trucks. Yet its status as an international importer-exporter is dwarfed by a country such as China, whose share of global advertising dollars, in the years from 1986 to 1996, grew 1,000 percent.

The 1990s have been a decade of frenetic economic globalization. A torrent of goods and capital has breached national boundaries that once held back the flows of international trade and financial investment. This headlong rush toward a global economy is underlain by an increasing concentration of wealth and power in corporations with worldwide reach. Since 1994 alone, $7.1 trillion worth of mergers and acquisitions have been transacted globally, with

---

2. Article by Jeff Gersh from *Amicus Journal,* Summer 1999. Copyright © *Amicus Journal.*
Reprinted with permission.

U.S. firms accounting for one-fifth of these. Today, according to David Korten, author of *The Post-Corporate World,* fifty-one of the largest global economies are corporations.

Globalization is facilitated by a spate of institutional and regulatory changes, in this country and abroad, aimed at liberalizing trade and investment practices. These changes reflect the contagious U.S. enchantment with freer markets and less government intervention. Crises in Asia and Latin America have stirred great debate about how to improve the workings of global financial systems. Yet the environmental dimensions of globalization are rarely discussed—an indication that world leaders and the communities they represent have not paused to question just what it is they are globalizing.

Background: Globalization and Development

Buried in the hoopla over celebrated business deals and skyrocketing trade and stock markets lies another reality As many as a billion people now live in absolute poverty. According to the United Nations, 20 percent of the populations of the world's poorest coun-

> *Because hunger and misery cannot afford to make the distinctions of the well-fed—to choose between cutting a tree or saving it— poverty is among the greatest environmental threats in the world.*

tries lack access to the most basic modern health care; 25 percent do not have adequate housing; 30 percent lack access to clean water. Because hunger and misery cannot afford to make the distinctions of the well-fed—to choose between cutting a tree or saving it—poverty is among the greatest environmental threats in the world. For moral reasons, let alone ecological reasons, it must be vanquished. And, in theory, economic development should increase the living standards of the have-nots, providing them with access to clean water, education, housing, and health care.

As early as 1987, the World Commission on Environment and Development (known as the Brundtland Commission) envisioned economic development as an achievable path to sustainability—that is, to an economic system that supports citizens at a decent standard of living without degrading the environment. But the Brundtland Commission added two caveats. Sustainability through economic development, the commission said, was only possible if environmentally benign technologies were developed and shared with poorer nations, and if the ecosystems of those nations were safeguarded.

The globalization trend is not living up to the Brundtland Commission's vision. Fifty years ago, President Harry Truman introduced into the diplomatic lexicon the phrase "undeveloped areas." Today, with savvy marketing and a nod to Wall Street, the world's poor countries are labeled "emerging markets"—economic butterflies breaking from their cocoons. Less developed nations include a labor force of some 4.4 billion people who occupy three-quarters of the globe's land area. These countries have traditionally tended to be net exporters of food, fuel, minerals, and other raw materials (see "Solving the Riddle of Development" *Amicus,* Summer 1998). For many of them, the rewards of participation in a global economy may seem theoretical at best. Since 1980, 100 nations have been either economically stagnant or in decline. On average, an African household today consumes one-fifth less than it did a quarter-century ago.

Other nations, such as China and Singapore, have caught fire, economically speaking. But rather than finding a new path of envi-

---

Can those who live in emerging markets endure "growth" long enough to enjoy its benefits?

---

ronmentally sustainable development, they are repeating the mistakes of the industrialized countries, and worse. In most of these nations, brisk economic development comes at great ecological expense, and environmental restoration has been postponed for some indefinite future. It has been estimated that the annual toll for environmental damage in China will reach $42 billion by the year 2000. Gold mining in the Philippines has cut large swaths of destruction in tropical forests, and many have charged that it is contaminating water sources. In Mexico, fifteen U.S. wood product firms have opened for business since NAFTA was approved in 1993. Boise Cascade has a five-year plan to send 20 million board feet of tropical hardwood to the United States; the International Paper Corporation helped push for passage of Mexico's Forest Reform Law, which eases environmental restrictions and provides for privatization of industrial forests.

Still, many economists counsel patience. If these emerging markets stay on the prescribed path of development, the argument goes, they will eventually raise their per capita incomes to the threshold at which economic and political capital takes an interest in environmental reforms. Mexico City is a case in point. Since December of 1998, journalist Julia Preston reports, exposure to pollutants such as automobile exhaust has sickened half the city's 18 million people with respiratory ailments. "Mexicans have other priorities. They see pollution as a luxury problem," sociologist Jose Luis Lezama told the reporter.

The theory is that Mexico City will begin to experience relief from polluted air once per capita incomes reach about $4,000. However, economist Eban Goodstein of Lewis and Clark College projects that at the country's annual growth rate of 4 percent, citizens will need to breathe bad air for another twenty-five years—for another generation. Globally, 1.3 billion people are exposed to air that does not meet the World Health Organization's minimum health standards. Can those who live in emerging markets endure "growth" long enough to enjoy its benefits?

As finance and trade become increasingly international, no one is minding the environmental store.

Moreover, while emissions of some pollutants are expected to decrease as incomes rise, others, such as carbon dioxide, continue to grow. In 1997, General Motors made a $1 billion deal with China to build 100,000 mid-sized automobiles a year. In a nation of 1.2 billion people, whose cities have been particularly accommodating to bicycles and mass transit, shifting toward reliance on the automobile will degrade air quality and boost emissions of greenhouse gases. Elsewhere around the world, the story is similar. According to the Institute for Policy Studies, since 1990 the World Bank has invested $9.4 billion on energy projects in developing nations. Over their lifetimes, these projects, which include large coal-fired power plants, will emit more carbon dioxide than is now produced by all the nations of the world.

Attorney Ruben Kraiem, NRDC trustee and board member of Mexico's Center for the Study of Sustainable Development, asks, "Do developing countries need to go through all the stages of development that the industrialized world has? Is there not a global imperative for saying we cannot afford to have poorer countries improve their standards of living by doing to their environments what we did to ours?"

Clearly, that global imperative exists. Just as clearly, most national leaders and businessmen are not paying attention. As finance and trade become increasingly international, no one is minding the environmental store.

Borderless Capital

The movement of finances from one country to another is not a new phenomenon. What has changed is the ease and speed of capital flows, in large measure the result of a worldwide trend toward eliminating policy barriers to foreign private investment. After the Depression, most countries enacted precautionary limits on the rights of individuals and corporations to purchase securities and other investments abroad. The Clinton administration, through the leadership of the Treasury Department, has championed liberalization of these barriers. Many developing nations, eager to court outside capital or under pressure from their debtors, have followed suit.

The consequences have been dramatic. From 1992 through 1995, mining investments in Brazil averaged $40 million annually. In 1996, $2.5 billion arrived. Why? The government erased its 49 percent limit on foreign participation in the mining industry. According to the World Watch Institute, between 1990 and 1996, private capital flows to emerging markets jumped from $44 billion to $244 billion.

Economic restructuring, properly administered, can have positive environmental benefits.

In itself, new financing is environmentally neutral. In the best of all possible worlds, much of this capital flowing into developing countries would be used to develop infrastructure and public transit systems and to finance a forward-looking manufacturing sector-including solar energy technology or drip irrigation systems, for example. In our own, less than perfect world, however, investors tend to follow paths they are familiar with, especially those likely to return a larger profit on a shorter time scale: real estate development, extraction of raw materials such as ore and timber, and expansion of traditional industrial capacity such as automobile manufacturing, among others. Worldwide, automakers can now produce 60 million cars a year; the current demand is only 44 million.

The ebb and flow of huge sums can have a dislocating effect on economies. In 1996, $93 billion landed in Indonesia, Malaysia, the Philippines, South Korea, and Thailand. One year later, investors pulled out $12 billion, a capital flight that contributed to a cascade of collapsing currencies and failed businesses. Enter the International Monetary Fund (IMF). In its role as global watchdog for monetary and economic policy, the IMF distributes large loans to needy nations in return for governments' promises to restructure their economies along lines approved by international economic orthodoxy (which is, by and large, U.S. economic orthodoxy).

"Structural adjustment" can impose stringent and painful require-
ments, such as rapid reduction of debts and deficits and cuts in government spending, including spending for education, health care,
and the environment.

Economic restructuring, properly administered, can have positive
environmental benefits such as ending harmful subsidies for the
looting of a nation's natural resources. But the IMF is not oriented
to environmental priorities. In 1998, for instance, the IMF, the
World Bank, the U.S. Treasury, and the government of Brazil
agreed to slice Brazil's budget for the environment by 66 percent.
That included the loss of some $62 million in foreign grants
intended to facilitate Indian land claims and to create urgently
needed protected areas. (This past January, the World Bank
announced that about a third of these funds would be restored—by
the bank's calculation, "virtually reestablishing the desired level of
financing.")

The race to pay back foreign loans under the stringent terms of
economic restructuring can also force nations into ill-conceived
development projects. Stephanie Freed of the Environmental
Defense Fund gives an example from Indonesia. In 1997, a fact-find-
ing mission led by U.S. Senator Max Baucus revealed that the
extraordinary forest fires of that year, which blackened the skies
over six countries and resulted in $1.3 billion in damages (not
including the catastrophic loss of trees), were "caused largely by
Indonesian and Malaysian timber companies clearing land for palm
oil plantations." Yet in 1998, the IMF pressed Indonesia to attract
new investment by removing barriers to foreign financing for palm
oil plantations.

Unfettered Trade

At the 1992 UN conference on the environment, held in Rio de
Janeiro, the nations of the world crafted an agenda for sustainability that included the goal of sustainable development via liberalized
trade. Says Victor Menotti, environment program director at the
San Francisco-based International Forum on Globalization, "This
was the strategic vision of Rio, whose tragic failure is now increasingly evident."

Like capital investment, trade in itself is environmentally neutral.
But environmental difficulties can arise when goods traverse large
geographic distances. The Boeing Corporation reports that air cargo
shipments have grown from 44 billion revenue ton-kilometers in
1985 to 123 billion in 1997. Each ton of air cargo requires nearly
fifty times as much energy as shipping. In practical terms, that
means that transporting 1 kilogram of tomatoes from, say, Spain to

Stockholm produces 1.7 kilograms of carbon dioxide emissions and 5 grams of nitrogen oxide, a losing proposition. But as long as fossil fuels and their pollutants continue to be highly subsidized around the world, the environmental costs of trade will not show up in the prices of the goods. They can perhaps only be measured in the melting of polar ice caps as global temperatures move upward.

Another problem with long-distance trade is that distance masks environmental costs. As University of Maryland ecological economist Herman Daly has pointed out, the U.S. public expresses outrage at the idea of opening the Arctic National Wildlife Refuge to oil exploration. Yet we seem relatively untroubled that oil imports from Nigeria—to name just one of our suppliers—are burdening the people of that country with a miserable environmental legacy of destroyed waterways and compromised immune systems.

And there is a further dimension to the environmental problems of trade: the international agreements and rules that govern it. "We are living through a major new phase in the evolution of the global economy, a new system of global governance," says Dan Seligman, director of the Sierra Club's Responsible Trade Campaign. He is referring to a system of institutions and initiatives that includes the Uruguay Round of the General Agreement on Tariffs and Trade (GATT); the World Trade Organization (WTO); and regional trade agreements such as the North American Free Trade Agreement (NAFTA), the Asia Pacific Economic Cooperation (APEC), and the Transatlantic Economic Partnership (TEP).

The problem with these conventions is that, with few exceptions, they do not incorporate environmental safeguards. Worse, as trade agreements have moved beyond their historical role of lowering tariffs, they are increasingly giving arbiters of trade disputes the power to eliminate non-tariff barriers to trade. And national health, safety, and environmental regulations are sometimes viewed as barriers to trade. In Seligman's view, the growing power of the international trading system is "a kind of solvent that's being poured on national regulatory systems. It is a form of stealth deregulation being enforced through international courts that lack any form of due process. This is a significant erosion of federal and state sovereignty."

In 1997, for instance, the United States-based Ethyl Corporation sued the government of Canada under NAFTA rules. Suspecting that a manganese-based fuel additive made by the company could harm public health, Canada had banned its import. The Ethyl Corporation argued that the ban had effectively "expropriated" its assets, and last summer it won a $13 million settlement.

Another cloud looming on the horizon is the possibility that the WTO may eventually consider scuttling the growing movement to promote eco-labeling programs, including certification of sustainably harvested wood (see "Building Forests, Growing Homes," *Amicus,* Spring 1997). According to the WTO's Agreement on Technical Barriers to Trade, nations may not show a prejudice against like products on the basis of the way they were produced. Indeed, *Business Week* reports that leaders in the timber industry have already warned the state of California and the cities of New York and Los Angeles that laws requiring the purchase of sustainably harvested wood might be contrary to international rules.

There is consensus among critics of trade agreements that the rules need to be revisited, overhauled, and democratized. Economist Herman Daly proposes that nations trying to account for environ-

---

In the last five years, globalization has hastened environmental destruction and eroded community self-determination.

---

mental costs—and charge the costs to those companies and consumers who incur them, rather than to the public at large—be permitted to place tariffs on trade with countries that do not. Economist Eban Goodstein suggests a modest across-the-board tax on trade, with the revenue used to create a "global environmental compliance fund." Goodstein calculates that a 1 percent tax on imports would generate about $40 billion a year, which could be distributed to developing countries to support environmental protection. Considering that estimates put the tab for providing clean water and sewers around the globe at only $9 billion, such a fund could have a significant impact. (And, to put the sum of $40 billion into perspective, the UN reports that Europeans eat $11 billion worth of ice cream every year.)

Other thinkers have gone still further than Daly and Goodstein. David Korten calls for "an entirely different kind of international agreement: affirming the rights of people to set their own health, safety, employment and environmental standards and to establish standards for regulating international corporations and financial flows." Michael Lerner, author of *The Politics of Meaning,* suggests that larger corporations should be required to apply for renewal of their charters every twenty years. The renewal process would require that each firm demonstrate "a history of social responsibility to the communities in which it operates."

Global Village?

Globalization has much in common with a powerful technology. It can be harmful or beneficial, depending on how it is used and on the policies that guide its implementation. In the last five years, globalization has hastened environmental destruction and eroded community self-determination. The world is not becoming a global village, but rather a system of corporate economies. Corporations today are relatively unconstrained by national borders or by regulatory structures intended to provide them with any guiding principle beyond that of making a buck. This is not the logical outcome of a free market, but rather the result of institutional choices. At best, nations and communities continue to misperceive the relationship between economic and ecological systems; at worst, they are ignoring it.

Consider what even a tiny portion of the wealth flying around the world today might do if investors made decisions based on a bottom line that values the environment properly.

In 1997, a conservation organization called Ecotrust, based in Portland, Oregon, partnered with the South Shore Bank of Chicago to create a hybrid in the world of banking. ShoreBank Pacific opened in Ilwaco, a coastal Washington town of 800 people in an area dotted with abandoned fish canneries and cut-over timber stands. The FDIC insured bank and its affiliated Enterprise Group provide clients with a combination of technical and marketing assistance and loans for sustainable development. With "ecodeposits" coming in from around the country, ShoreBank is certainly in business to make a profit, but it "also has a more complex vision. "No other bank has conservation-based development as its core business mission. We're training our lending officers to do an environmental assessment at the same time they do a credit assessment," says president John Delf. He projected that the bank would soon have about $15 million. "It's nothing to be embarrassed about," he says, "but it's small."

Many U.S. citizens today are unwittingly contributing to the destructive power of globalization by investing in mutual funds and in their "local" banks, whose only moral imperative is to seek the highest return. If just a fraction of those monies were to start finding their way into ecobanks, and even standard socially responsible mutual funds, there might be more Delfs in the world, with more capital to show for their efforts.

Every once in a while, I see a faded bumper sticker on a rusted car or old pickup that reads: "Think globally. Act locally." That charge is no longer sufficient. We must be prepared to think and act at both scales now.

Killing Them Softly[3]

BY JENNIFER SCARLOTT
E: THE ENVIRONMENTAL MAGAZINE, JANUARY/FEBRUARY 2000

Although a recent *New York Times* piece claimed that wild tigers have made a "remarkable recovery," a quick look at the real numbers gives a more accurate picture of the challenge this magnificent species faces at the brink of extinction.

There were an estimated 100,000 wild tigers in Asia at the turn of the century. One hundred years later, their numbers have declined by 95 percent, and only 5,000 to 7,000 tigers are estimated to survive, approximately 4,000 of them in India. While there were eight subspecies in 1900, there are only five now. Conservationists the world over give the wild tiger anywhere from 10 to 25 years unless sustained emergency action is taken.

Back in the early 1970s, the picture was even worse. Decades of wholesale slaughter and habitat destruction had dropped Indian tiger numbers to an estimated 1,700. Backed by a million-dollar pledge from the World Wildlife Fund, the Government of India launched Project Tiger in 1973. Its objectives were two-fold: to "ensure the maintenance of a viable population of tigers" and "preserve for all time, areas of biological importance as a national heritage for the benefit, education and enjoyment of the people." A ban on tiger hunting was finally imposed and entire villages were moved out of areas designated as sanctuaries. For the next 15 years or so, tigers responded vigorously, and Project Tiger was lauded and emulated all over the world.

Relief turned to panic in the late 1980s, when censuses of tiger populations began to reveal that many were "missing." In fact, tigers were nowhere near as numerous as the Indian government reported. Investigations revealed that tigers were being trapped, poisoned and shot at an estimated rate of one per day to provide parts for the global black market trade in Chinese traditional medicine. By this time, China had virtually wiped out its own tiger population, having long viewed them as "pests." Tigers were also killed in growing numbers by farmers living on the borders of tiger forests.

But in the last decade, another formidable threat to tiger survival joined poaching and population pressure: runaway economic globalization. The tiger is now up against dams, mines, roads, tourism

---

3.   Reprinted with permission from *E: The Environmental Magazine,* Subscription Department: P.O. Box 2047, Marion, OH 43306; telephone (815) 734-1242. Subscriptions are $20 per year.

projects, thermal plants, cement factories, chemical effluents and commercial forestry projects, all being built in India on a massive scale.

As Bittu Sahgal, a long-time tiger activist and editor of India's largest wildlife magazine, *Sanctuary,* puts it: "Were poaching and population the limit of the problem, I would say the tiger could be saved through a combination of education, protection and consultation with communities. Unfortunately, industrialists and international bureaucrats are developing the tiger out of existence."

> *"Unfortunately, industrialists and international bureaucrats are developing the tiger out of existence."*
> —Bittu Sahgal, a tiger activist.

The World Bank, which has an enormous presence in India, is working on two tracks. It funds numerous economic infrastructure development projects which, activists say, threaten fragile ecosystems and tiger habitat throughout the country. At the same time, they add, it throws up a "green" smokescreen of concern for biodiversity.

Hazaribagh ("Land of a Thousand Tigers") National Park in central India provides corridors vital to migrating tigers and elephants, which coal mines run by Coal India threaten to disconnect. Aided by World Bank funds, over 495 new coal mines are being added to those currently in operation.

In the Indian state of Bihar, the World Bank is financing the Kotku Dam, which will drown the best forests of a tiger reserve called Palamau.

In Andhra Pradesh, a "Forestry Project" funded by the World Bank will convert tiger habitat to a monoculture designed to boost commerce rather than biodiversity. Bulldozing old-growth trees will make way for money-making species such as eucalyptus, teak and bamboo. "Tigers will no longer be able to live in such altered forests," says Saghal. In Madhya Pradesh, an area of critical importance to the survival of tigers in India, the Bank may invest more than $200 million over a 10-year period, "for development of the forestry sector."

According to Ashish Kothari, a founding member of the Pune-based Kalpavriksh Environment Action Group, which has been working on conservation and development for 20 years, "The World Bank has greatly aided an uncontrolled 'development' process which treats all of nature as raw materials. Even national parks and sanctuaries are being sacrificed for dams, power plants, highways and tourism complexes."

An arm of the Bank plans to spend $90 million on something called the "India Ecodevelopment Project," to "conserve biodiversity" near parks and sanctuaries. But according to a number of Indian environmental groups, pouring millions into seven protected areas, including five Project Tiger reserves, is not halting but spurring destruction of the forests and the local peoples' way of life.

Dr. Ravi Chellam, a scientist and research coordinator with the Wildlife Institute of India in Dehra Dun, bemoans the World Bank's self-imposed and disingenuous role as a green superhero. "In Kalakad-Mundanthurai Tiger Reserve in southern Tamil Nadu, much of the Bank's money is thrown at shoddily-constructed, unnecessary projects. It has always amazed me that in the name of conserving nature, we actually destroy it by bringing in tons of concrete and steel!"

Some tiger advocates do praise the Bank's role. Dr. V. K. Melkani, field director of the Kalakud Tiger Reserve portion of the Ecodevelopment Project, points to the Bank's "biodiversity enhancement" agenda which, he says, "provides us with an opportunity to test a new tool for forest protection."

The Bank itself declined to comment directly about its role in tiger conservation. Instead, it provided *E* with the following statement: "The Bank's current environmental strategy aims to introduce environmental concerns into all aspects of the Bank's work through 'do no harm' policies to avoid and mitigate the negative impacts of infrastructure, power and other development activities."

The view from most environmentalists in India is that if the Bank doesn't change course, it will only be a matter of time for the tiger. Other threats to its survival seem serious, but manageable. Commercial development just might do what the poachers' snares and farmers' guns have not.

Bibliography

Books

Aristide, Jean-Bertrand. *Eyes of the Heart: Seeking a Path for the Poor in the Age of Globalization*. Monroe, ME: Common Courage Press, 2000.

Barber, Benjamin R. *Jihad vs. McWorld*. New York: Ballantine Books, 1995.

French, Hilary. *Vanishing Borders: Protecting the Planet in the Age of Globalization*. New York: W.W. Norton & Company, 2000.

Friedman, Thomas L. *The Lexus and the Olive Tree*. New York: Farrar, Straus, Giroux, 1999.

Giddens, Anthony. *Runaway World: How Globalization is Reshaping Our Lives*. London, Profile Books, 1999.

Gray, John. *False Dawn: The Delusions of Globals Capitalism*. New York: New Press, 1998.

Held, David, et al. *Global Transformations: Politics, Economics and Culture*. Cambridge, UK: Polity Press, 1999.

Herod, Andrew, Gearoid O. Tuathail, and Susan M. Roberts (Editors). *An Unruly World?: Globalization, Governance and Geography*. New York: Routledge, 1998.

Hirst, Paul, and Grahame Thompson. *Globalization in Question: The International Economy and the Possibilities of Governance*. Cambridge, Massachusett: Blackwell Publishers, 1996.

Jameson, Fredric, and Masao Miyoshi (Editors). *The Cultures of Globalization*. Durham, North Carolina: Duke University Press, 1998.

Kalb, Don, Marco Van Der Land, and Richard Staring (Editors). *The Ends of Globalization: Bringing Society Back In*. Lanham, Maryland: Rowman & Littlefield Publishers, 2000.

Micklethwait, John, and Adrian Wooldridge. *A Future Perfect: The Challenge and Hidden Promise of Globalization*. New York: Times Books, 2000.

Mittelman, James H. *The Globalization Syndrome*. Princeton, New Jersey: Princeton University Press, 2000.

Polanyi, Karl. *The Great Transformation*. New York: Farrar & Rinehart, Inc., 1944.

Rodrik, Dani. *Has Globalization Gone Too Far?* Washington, DC: Institute of International Economics, 1997.

Sassen, Saskia. *Globalization and Its Discontents: Essays on the New Mobility of People and Money*. New York: New Press, 1998.

Vayrynen, Raimo (Editor). *Globalization and Global Governance*. Lanham, Maryland: Rowman & Littlefield Publishers, 1999.

Wallach, Lori, and Michelle Sforza. *Whose Trade Organization?: Corporate Globalization and the Erosion of Democracy*. Washington, DC: Public Citizen Foundation, 1999.

Additional Periodical Articles with Abstracts

More information on globalization can be found in the following articles. Readers who require a more comprehensive selection are advised to consult *Reader's Guide Abstracts* and other H. W. Wilson indexes.

NGOing Global. Sherle R. Schwenninger. *Civilization* Feb. 2000

Sherle R. Schwenninger discusses the background and influence of nongovernmental organizations (NGOs) in today's global environment. Although NGOs have contributed to the improvement of conditions on a global scale, Schwenninger questions their influence in the future. Despite their strengths—including a base of nonpartisan participants and funding sources drawn from the richest classes, NGOs can only provide a grassroots "soft governance" in a world that is increasingly in need of more structured governmental systems. The very nature of NGOs, particularly their lack of democratic accountability, prohibits them from taking on a more structured role.

Power Passport: Hoping to Tap Opportunities Back Home, Asian Women Seek MBAs at Chicago Biz Schools. Margaret Littman. *Crain's Chicago Business* v. 22 p15+ Sep. 27, 1999

In an effort to make the most of opportunities in their home countries, Asian women are increasingly enrolling in MBA courses at Chicago business schools. The improving status of women in business in Asia is the result of increased international competition, globalization, and the growing adoption of the free market in such nations as China. The number of Asian-born women taking the Graduate Management Admission Test and enrolling in U.S. business schools has recently been growing faster than the number of U.S. women doing so.

Etiquette Tips for Today's Global Economy: What to Know Before You Go. Mary Kay Metcalf. *Direct Marketing* v. 61 pp22-3 Mar. 1999

Noting that increased globalization of business has brought with it a corresponding increase in the importance of etiquette, Mary Kay Metcalf offers a primer on a sampling of the correct practices to follow in foreign countries. Awkward situations can often be diffused by proper handling of local customs and protocol. For instance, one should never assume that a foreign counterpart can speak English. Other rules include the protocol for making introductions, the different concepts of time held by citizens of different countries, and the use of business cards.

Dueling Globalizations: A Debate Between Thomas L. Friedman and Ignacio Ramonet. *Foreign Policy* pp110-27 Fall 1999

This article is actually a debate between Thomas L. Friedman and Ignacio

Ramonet over the issues raised by globalization. Friedman argues that globalization, which is based on integration, has replaced the Cold War as the
new international system. It has its own dominant culture that tends to have
an homogenizing effect and facilitates the spread of Americanization.
According to Ramonet, globalization is not as benign as Friedman portrays
it. Rather, globalization is aiding the implosion of multinational communities
around the globe. In addition, it is based mainly on money and thus ignores
the social needs of humanity and creates an environment in which only the
strongest can survive. The writers are given an opportunity to respond to
each others' arguments.

Globalization and the Return of History. Emma Rothschild. *Foreign Policy* pp106-16 Summer 1999

The writer discusses the history of internationalization and globalizatiᵤᵤ.
Depicted as a condition of the present and the future, globalization possesses
a history that should be taken into account when discussing present-day politics. Globalization is associated with, among other things, new and
unequaled technologies, international capital markets, and just-in-time
deliveries across vast distances, but it is a concept that can be examined in
the perspective of the economic and social history of international relations.
The period that began around 1770 and ended in the Napoleonic wars is of
particular relevance to the contemporary world, and it was a period when
private corporations, most notably the Dutch, English, French, and Swedish
East India Companies, played a decisive part in internationalization.

World Trade: Rewriting the Rules. Deepak Gopinath. *Institutional Investor* v. 34 pp51-54 Feb. 2000

After the failure of the December 1999 round of global trade talks, held in
Seattle, Washington, many people are trying to explain the meaning and
symbolism of the protest demonstrations. These events represent a serious
danger to globalization, the main tenets of which were enshrined in the 1990
Washington consensus. A number of disenchanted developing countries see
the process of liberalization as designed to be of greatest benefit to richer
countries. Furthermore, the leaders of less-well-developed countries state
that they do not want to be dictated to either by developed world governments *or* by well-intentioned first-world citizen protests. According to Juan
Somavia, director general of the International Labor Organization, the activity on the streets of Seattle was a response to the insecurity and uncertainty
created by the global economy. Officials of the World Trade Organization
admit that the message of the demonstrations cannot be ignored.

People Power. Barry Came. *Maclean's* pp220-2 Jan. 1, 2000

The demonstrations against the World Trade Organization's meeting in
Seattle, Washington, showed how much power nongovernmental organizations (NGOs) have gained in recent years. The groups, which are now so
numerous that the UN has an office just to keep record of them, have many
different and particular aims, but they are all united in wanting to create an
"international civil society." The writer discusses the organization and growing political clout of NGOs.

The Orient Effect: Why All Things Asian Are Cool with Kids. Glenn Chin and Ed Caffyn. *Marketing* v. 105 p41 Feb. 21, 2000

According to the authors, Asia's prominence as a global cultural force is on the rise. Western culture appears to be losing its grip and is no longer the predominant force for communicating what is cool. On the streets, the so-called Orient Effect can be seen in fashion boutiques and in popular music, which is developing a healthy Asian profile. The Asian influence is also apparent in the cinemas where Japanese animation has moved into the mainstream. North American culture is exhausted from its preeminence over the past century, whereas on the other side of the world, globalization is in full swing. The authors suggest that the Orient Effect will continue for the foreseeable future, and so marketers should consider going East for a possible glimpse at future Western trends.

The World Trade Organization? Stop World Take Over. William K. Tabb. *Monthly Review* v. 51 pp1-12 Jan. 2000

William K. Tabb reports that on November 30, 1999, when the World Trade Organization (WTO) opened its third round of ministerial meetings, tens of thousands of protestors gathered from all over the world in Seattle, Washington, to denounce the organization. He notes that approximately 800 grass-roots organizations from over 75 countries called for resistance to the increasing power of corporate greed, charging that the WTO's rules and procedures are undemocratic and serve to marginalize further the majority of the world's people, who are enmeshed in the instability and social degradation of the process of globalization without social control. He points out that although the WTO portrays the framework of trade as maximizing self-interest through economic exchange, it is in fact a trade regime that maximizes the interests of the giant corporations. He provides details of the origins of the WTO; how the organization operates; and why protestors seek revolutionary change from transnational-corporation rule of the world system of trade.

Globalization and American Power. Kenneth N. Waltz. *National Interest* pp46-56 Spring 2000

Kenneth N. Waltz questions the reach and irreversibility of globalization. He recounts globalizers' arguments that the "losers" will want to imitate the "winners" and points out that this lack of individual initiative would mean the end of autonomous nation states. While globalizers often concede that the nation state is indeed losing sovereignty, Waltz provides evidence to the contrary. The world is less an interdependent whole based on economic relations, he argues, than a system of inequality, where the rich countries—particularly the U.S.—dictate the rules. The U.S. holds this position because of its strong nation state. Weak states lead to economic turmoil, as we have seen in Russia after the breakdown of the authoritarian Soviet regime. Thus politics hold more sway in determining the path of globalization than economics do.

Policing Utopia: The Military Imperatives of Globalization. Andrew J. Bacevich. *National Interest* pp5-13 Summer 1999

Ignoring visions of self-regulating peace and prosperity, the U.S. defense establishment, according to Andrew J. Bacevich, seeks to stifle opposition to the U.S. version of globalization by institutionalizing its own military supremacy. Under the doctrine of the Clinton administration, the Pentagon aims to maintain a level of military dominance that will thwart any serious challenge. In the future, the military establishment will not merely respond to events but assert itself proactively to "shape" the international environment. It is able to wield its military power freely in the conditions of the post-Cold War era, but the inclination to actually use force stems from the particular worldview that President Bill Clinton and his chief lieutenants have outlined. At the core of this approach to strategy is the notion of globalization, now an all-embracing rationale for the role of the U.S. in the world.

Flip Flop. Jon Henley. *New Republic* v. 222 p24 Jan. 3, 2000

McDonald's is hoping an advertising campaign can reverse the rising wave of anti-American sentiment in France that is targeting the fast-food chain. French farmers are protesting against what they see as an "ever-encroaching U.S. hegemony," ever since the U.S. government enforced crippling import tariffs on French produce in response to a European ban on hormone-enhanced American beef. Jose Bove, the French sheep farmer and cheese maker who served a 20-day jail sentence after vandalizing an unfinished McDonald's outlet, sees the chain as representative of three evils: globalization, industrially produced food, and America. Bove seems to have the support of most of his countrymen, including Prime Minister Lionel Jospin, who are increasingly worried about the food they are consuming. In response, McDonald's has introduced an advertising campaign making fun of Americans and stressing that McDonald's France uses French produce.

Fund and Games. Alexandra Starr. *New Republic* v. 222 p14 Mar. 27, 2000

Alexandra Starr declares that perhaps the most important national economic position in the world, that of managing director of the IMF, has been sacrificed at the altar of diplomatic affirmative action. For years, the top jobs at the world's major international institutions have been allotted according to a strict system. The presidency of the World Bank goes to an American, the secretary-general of the UN is plucked from the Third World, and the top slots at NATO and the IMF are reserved for the major European powers. Although the head of the IMF has usually been French, this year, with a British head of NATO, an Italian president of the European Commission, and a Frenchman slated to head the European Central Bank, German chancellor Gerhard Schroder wants to claim the IMF for Germany. The problems with the German candidate and the system of allocating the job are examined.

Beyond the Nation State. Ulrich Beck. *New Statesman* v. 128 Dec. 6, 1999

The writer discusses the effect that globalization has had on the old politics, and he argues that there is now a need for a new form of politics. The process of globalization is not only getting rid of the restraints caused by trade unions but also the restraints imposed by the nation-state. Politicians do not comprehend that their calls for ever more open markets are threatening their own lifeblood. Transnational corporations first moved jobs to places where they would be cheapest. They then used computers to break down and disperse goods and services and to produce them through a division of labor that caused national and corporate labels to become illusory. They then played off one country against another in order to find the best infrastructure and cheapest fiscal conditions. The only way that the nation-state can survive is if it adjusts to globalization in every area, including military affairs, the law, and economics.

The Citizens of Nowhere in Arabia's Hong Kong. Christian Caryl. *New Statesman* v. 129 pp32-3 Apr. 3, 2000

Christian Caryl writes that Dubai appears to be the perfect example of globalization at work, with great multiculturalism, laissez-faire economics, and vestigial taxes and tariffs. Dubai would seem to be an advertisement for globalization as the inevitable triumph of Western-style laissez-faire economics and tolerance, but it could just as easily serve the opposite purpose. Only 15 percent or so of the population of Dubai are local citizens, and the result implies a surrender of political rights in the name of economic betterment. The economic libertarianism of Dubai contrasts sharply with the political despotism of its politics, as decision-making in the emirate starts and stops with Sheikh Maktoum.

What's Wrong with This Picture of Nationalism. Serge Schmemann. *New York Times* pIV1 Feb. 21, 1999

Serge Schmemann argues that the rise in ethnic conflicts and the establishment of many new nation states carved from larger countries is not surprising. Ethnic hatreds are ancient and existed for centuries, even during the Cold War, but the tensions caused by the Cold War often superseded ethnic conflicts. When the Cold War ended, small regions no longer needed to stay under the wings of larger countries, and the rise in globalization of the marketplace has made nationhood a must for small regions hoping to compete for resources. Many regions recognized this need and therefore resolved ethnic conflicts peacefully. Schmemann finds that the rise in ethnic-related violence usually results from a difficult transition to democracy, when politicians use xenophobia as a uniting platform because no other familiar structure still stands. Thus the end of the Cold War did not necessarily release these ancient hatreds. They were there and used only as a one method for adjusting to a new, globalized world.

Globalization of R&D Enters New Stage as Firms Learn to Integrate Technology Operations on World Scale. Manuel Serapio, Donald Dalton, and Phyllis Genther Yoshida. *Research Technology Management* v. 43 pp2-4 Jan./Feb. 2000

Multinational corporations from the U.S., Europe, and Asia are increasing the rate at which they invest in overseas research and development (R&D).

In excess of 100 international businesses have now acquired multiple laboratories abroad that are used as a source of new technologies. The authors discuss various aspects of this trend, including the integration of domestic and overseas R&D facilities, the increase in global R&D mergers and acquisitions, the use of direct investment in R&D as an opportunity to learn about and develop new technologies, and the success of technology centers in emerging markets.

The Three Horsemen of Globalization. Monte Paulsen. *Salon* Dec. 2, 1999

Monte Paulsen examines the increasing collaboration of the three major world governing bodies: the World Trade Organization (WTO), the International Monetary Fund (IMF), and the World Bank. As protests against the WTO raged in Seattle, Washington, the other two organization formalized another step toward consolidating power between themselves and the WTO. Paulsen recounts the history of collaboration amongst the three organizations and reviews the negative aspects of such an conglomeration. Meanwhile, he points out, criticism of each group individually is also rising.

Becoming Evangelists of Justice: What Will It Take to Build a Humane Global Economy? Richard Parker. *Sojourners* v. 28 pp36-9 Sep./ Oct. 1999

As America enters the 21st century, it faces a number of economic problems that correspond to those it faced at the beginning of the 20th century, namely: overproduction and overcapacity in critical industries, unprecedented mergers and acquisitions, unalloyed financial market growth, and soaring income and wealth inequality. At the beginning of the century, a dedicated community of reformers set out to prove that the cruel Social Darwinism of the times could be brought to heel by a citizenry committed to building a nation that would be both democratic and economically successful. This movement began as an often inchoate welter of citizen groups, was multiclass, and included key elements in America's religious community. It shows us that the conditions that we face in the so-called new global economy are not new and that a coalition that seeks to end the impoverishment of the American middle classes as well as the suffering of the poor is required to truly transform America.

The Lines That Separate Us: Borders in a "Borderless" World. David Newman. *Tikkun* pp19-21 May/June 2000

The myth of globalization is that it is a global phenomenon. While the world may be undergoing a process of territorial reconfiguration, and the relative impact of a boundary as a barrier to the movement of goods, information, and people may be changing, the boundaries themselves are far from disappearing. The Western story of a world without borders does not include those seen as "undesirable" or threatening. People living in rural India or rural China, along with hundreds of thousands of refugees have no experience of a borderless world. It should not be assumed that a globalized world is a world without borders and that all differences will disappear in such a world.

Workers of the World, Speak Up. Rich Little. *Time Europe* v. 155 June 26, 2000

The debate over globalization and the impact on the everyday lives of people rages on without the aid of the voices of factory workers—the frontlines of many globalized companies. Rich Little makes a case for listening to these voices in order to devise long-term goals that are of concern to the workers. Students may protest on behalf of sweatshop workers, but their solutions (a rise in wages) address only some of the concerns voiced by workers when the Global Alliance—a coalition comprising multinational companies, foundations, nongovernmental organizations, and the World Bank—began interviews with them. Along with wages, workers (disproportionately young people) wanted training in life skills, family and labor laws, and management skills. They see factory work as an opportunity where previously there were no choices. Since the percentage of young people is rising, Little writes, we need to start listening to their voices.

The Migration Boom. Stephen Castles and Patrick Brownlee. *UNESCO Sources* Jan. 1998

This article is a report put out by a United Nations agency to review the current standing of migration. While migration is nothing new, globalization has seemed to speed up its volume and scope. International migration has caused the formation of community links across the globe as families get separated, and has transformed cities into multicultural centers. Although some people move for political reasons (such as refugees), the majority of migrants today move to find better jobs and living standards. The authors characterize the general pattern of migration, discuss the reasons for the growing numbers of female migrants, explain the reluctance of countries providing migrants to stop the process, and describe the impact of migration on the culture and identity of nations.

Hell, no. We Won't Trade. Dori Jones Yang. *U.S. News & World Report* Nov. 1, 1999

The writer notes that just a decade ago world trade was unassailable, yet today thousands march in protest of the World Trade Organization. While the protestors vary in their specific goals and methods, Ralph Nader and his group, Public Citizen, seeks to unite the opposition. The author questions why, now that the U.S. and the world economies are faring so well, opposition has grown so fierce. She lists several reasons for the timing and opines that resistance will go nowhere, at the moment, because politicians and well-placed citizens continue to support world trade.

Attack of the Killer Kapitalists. Lenora Todaro. *Village Voice* Nov. 24-30, 1999

Activists who gathered in Seattle, Washington, to protest the trade talks of the World Trade Organization (WTO) are drawn from diverse sources, but they almost all agree that the WTO should not be allowed to superimpose its global standards over nation states' own laws. Todaro recounts some instances in which the WTO ruled over trade disputes between countries, and she lists some of the WTOs retorts to detractors. The protestors, Todaro notes, are an organized lot. They marched on Seattle by way of 18 rest stops, where they provided teach-ins to educate the public about global issues. While most protest groups are individually rather small and therefore have formed coalitions, the AFL-CIO, America's labor union, is very large. Its members contributed a sizeable presence at the protests. The protesters are really opposed to global corporate domination.

Index